HOW TO TRACE YOUR FAMILY TREE

HOW TO TRACE YOUR FAMILY TREE

A Complete and
Easy to Understand Guide
for the Beginner

AMERICAN GENEALOGICAL
RESEARCH INSTITUTE STAFF

NEW YORK LONDON TORONTO SYDNEY AUCKLAND

A MAIN STREET BOOK
PUBLISHED BY DOUBLEDAY
a division of Bantam Doubleday Dell Publishing Group, Inc.
1540 Broadway, New York, New York 10036

MAIN STREET BOOKS, DOUBLEDAY, and the portrayal of a building with a tree are trademarks of Doubleday, a division of Bantam Doubleday Dell Publishing Group, Inc.

Originally published by
American Genealogical Research Institute,
A Division of Heritage Press, Inc.

ISBN: 0-385-09885-5
Library of Congress Catalog Card Number 73-88881

PRINTED IN THE UNITED STATES OF AMERICA
22 23 21

CONTENTS

Foreword **vii**

Chapter *Page*

1 **Introduction** *William A. Roskey* **1**

2 **How to Organize Your Findings** *Arthur S. Wortman* **7**
Pedigree charts. ▪ Coding system. ▪ Individual work sheets. ▪ Family group work sheets. ▪ Miscellaneous file.

3 **History for Genealogists** *William A. Roskey* **15**
Interrelationship of history and genealogy. ▪ Calendar change. ▪ Boundary changes. ▪ History of American immigration.

4 **You and Your Family As Research Sources**
Ann I. Mahoney **42**
Where and how to begin research. ▪ Correspondence with relatives. ▪ Interviewing relatives. ▪ Diaries and other family records to search.

5 **Printed Sources** *AGRI Staff* **54**
Use of the library. ▪ Classification. ▪ General bibliography. ▪ Surname and heraldry bibliography. ▪ Periodical indexes. ▪ Genealogical data sources.

6 **Local Records** *Paul C. Larsen* **76**
Visiting the courthouse. ▪ Records by mail. ▪ Official court records. ▪ Vital statistics. ▪ Probate records. ▪ Wills. ▪ The Shrieve Case.

7 **State Records** *AGRI Staff* **89**
State-by-state list of where to obtain vital records (birth, marriage, and death data). ▪ State-by-state list of genealogical libraries or archives.

8 Federal Government Research Sources
Paul C. Larsen 136
National Archives. ▪ Use of records. ▪ Census material. ▪ The Mortality Census Schedules. ▪ The Pension Records. ▪ Pension Payment Records. ▪ The Bounty-Land Records. ▪ The Passenger Arrival Lists. ▪ Miscellaneous Records.

9 Miscellaneous Records—Churches, Cemeteries, Lodges, Etc. *Ann I. Mahoney* 15[illegible]
How and where to research newspaper files, records of private organizations, institutional and church records, and cemetery gravestones.

10 Heraldry *J. Charles Thompson* 164
Armory and Armigers. ▪ Designing your own arms. ▪ Protecting your arms. ▪ The tradition of arms ▪ The Scrope vs. Grosvenor case. ▪ Heraldry through history ▪ "Bogus" arms. ▪ Arms in the United States. ▪ Heraldic achievement. ▪ Terms used in heraldry.

11 Hereditary, Patriotic, and Genealogical Societies
Ernest F. Kendall 183

Bibliography 189

FOREWORD

This is a beginner's guide to a fascinating, exciting, and fast-growing hobby. For a long time the American Genealogical Research Institute has, in its publications, spoken glowingly of the many rewards of genealogy. As a result, we daily receive letters from people all over the country which say, in essence, "Yes, all well and good. But how do I *begin?*" We attempted to answer this question in our previous publications, but, unfortunately, space limitations prevented us from treating the topic in the depth that it demands. The purpose, then, of this book is to explicitly answer this question.

All too many of the previously published "how-to" books have tended to assume that the reader knows more about genealogy than he actually does. As a result, the novice genealogist has been lost in unfamiliar terms, confusing case histories, and vague directions. Naturally, the beginner feels frustrated. This volume, on the other hand, contends that a "how-to" book is for those individuals—young and old—who have no previous knowledge of genealogy. This book, designed specifically for the novice, answers the basic question, "How do I begin?"

Readers of previous AGRI publications will recognize some of the material. In addition to writing and compiling much new information for this volume, we have reprinted some of the best material on the subject from earlier publications. This reprinted material is particularly useful to the amateur genealogist as a basic reference. It has been a great help to us in achieving the goal of this book: to put between two covers all the rudimentary knowledge that a person needs to know to begin his genealogy.

1

INTRODUCTION

William A. Roskey

There is a moral and philosophical respect for our ancestors which elevates the character and improves the heart. Next to the sense of religious duty and moral feeling, I hardly know what should bear with stronger obligation on a liberal and enlightened mind than a consciousness of an alliance with excellence which is departed, and a consciousness, too, that in its act and conduct, and even in the sentiments and thoughts, it may be actively operating on the happiness of those who come after it.

DANIEL WEBSTER

Ever since H.G. Wells published his fabulous novel, *The Time Machine,* men have shared his dream of a machine to journey into the past. Time and events in time have shaped our civilization, and therefore shaped us—our hopes and aspirations, our values and customs, even our language. The very blood of men who have long since turned to dust flows in our veins, and this knowledge has intrigued many philosophers. Ralph Waldo Emerson wrote that "We are the children of many sires, and every drop of blood in us in its turn betrays its ancestor."

Therefore, it is no wonder that the past fascinates us, and that, sometimes, when we are alone with our own hearts, in flights of fantasy, we dream of a wonderous vehicle that will take us backward in time. Unfortunately, we do not have, very probably will never have, something built of wires, tubes, transistors, and sophisticated electronic devices which will do the job for us. But we do have the words and thoughts of those who have gone before us. These, coupled with our own imagination, are probably the closest we will ever get to time travel—the closest we will ever get to meeting our ancestors face-to-face, and experiencing the events that they did.

The science of electronics will not help us here, but the science of genealogy will. The word itself comes from two Greek words meaning birth and study, and is at least as old as the epistles of St. Paul, where it appears in the original Greek. The actual practice of genealogy is nearly as old as man himself, and perhaps the most widely read genealogy begins:

> This is the book of the generations of Adam. When God created man, he made him in the likeness of God. Male and female he created them, and he blessed them and named them Man when they were created. When Adam had lived a hundred and thirty years, he became the father of a son in his own likeness, after his image, and named him Seth. The days of Adam after he became the father of Seth were eight hundred years; and he had other sons and daughters. Thus all the days that Adam lived were nine hundred and thirty years; and he died.
>
> When Seth had lived a hundred and five years, he became the father of Enosh. Seth lived after the birth of Enosh eight hundred and seven years, and had other sons and daughters. Thus all the days of Seth were nine hundred and twelve years; and he died.
>
> When Enosh had lived ninety years, he became the father of Kenan. Enosh lived after the birth of Kenan eight hundred and fifteen years, and had other sons and daughters. Thus all the days of Enosh were nine hundred and five years; and he died.
>
> When Kenan had lived seventy years, he became the father of Ma-hal-alel. Kenan lived after the birth of Ma-hal-alel eight hundred and forty years, and had other sons and daughters. Thus all the days of Kenan were nine hundred and ten years; and he died.

This particular passage from the Old Testament continues

with Adam's line up through the sons of Noah who were Shem, Ham, and Japheth.

Virtually all societies have kept genealogical records, whether oral, written, or both. However, up until as recently as the sixteenth century, genealogy was almost exclusively concerned with the rulers or nobility of the various civilizations. The Greek and Roman rulers used genealogy to "prove" that they were descended from gods and goddesses. Numerous other nationalities including Egyptians, Chinese, Japanese, and many Europeans (the English among them) used it to record the succession of their heads of state.

By way of an interesting sidelight concerning royal genealogies, Irish monastic chroniclers of the sixth and seventh centuries "traced" the descent of their kings back to Milesius (King of Spain around 1000 B.C.), then through Noah back to Adam himself. This, of course, is absolutely impossible, although these genealogies are considered to be accurate enough back as far as 600 A.D. The rest is pure embroidery.

This brings up an interesting point for the beginning genealogist—just how far back *can* a man reasonably expect to go? Unfortunately, the answer has to be that it depends. It is determined by many factors, some of them peculiar to individual families and others related to world history. For example, the national origin of an individual doing a genealogy will define certain parameters even before he begins. To examine specific cases, it may be possible for someone of Middle Eastern extraction to trace himself back to the seventh century, whereas it is highly unlikely for someone whose ancestors came from Indo-China to be able to go back further than two hundred years. No one of European extraction can go beyond the third or fourth century (and only a handful of royal lines can go back that far), but someone whose origin is in India may be able to go back more than a thousand years.

The above figures, it must be noted, presuppose optimum conditions. The great majority of us cannot hope to obtain results like this. We are a society of record keepers now, but this is a very recent development as far as history goes. No doubt the genealogists of the future will have an extremely easy time of it with our telephone directories, drivers' licenses, voters registration lists, and so on. The ponderous files of the Internal Revenue Service alone will practically complete their pedigree charts for them. But this doesn't help us now. We "old-time genealogists" will have to do it the hard way.

What kind of records do we have to work with? Of course, one of the first things that comes to mind is census listings. National censuses are valuable tools indeed for the genealogist. But the first census held in any European country was not until as recently as 1085, and although it is probably numerically accurate, it is not specific enough. We speak here of the *Domesday Book*, the census commissioned by William the Conqueror. It was an ambitious project, the object being to record every field, wood, domestic animal, and human being in all of England. This was duly accomplished, but very few of the 283,342 people counted have their names listed.

At any rate, although this was the first European census, *regular* census-taking in England did not begin until 1801. The United States began regular censuses in 1790, and Scotland in 1755. Many other nations have since begun their own census programs, but in a genealogical sense, these are extremely recent records. However, there are still tax records, land records, wills, birth and death records, marriage records, military records, and other similar information that virtually all governments have kept. Depending on the information we begin with, the national origin of our ancestors, and the type of records we are searching, it is, of course, possible to go further back than census records, but oftentimes a good deal of patience, perseverance, and just plain luck is required.

In general, record keeping did not begin in earnest until the sixteenth century, but it has become increasingly more extensive as the years have gone by. It is possible to trace your own line back prior to 1500, but to accomplish this, you must almost of necessity be related at that point to one of the great families (the nobility) of that age. The ordinary man of those far-off days was not only unable to write his own name, but never had his name written down by anyone else.

While it is a fascinating subject, tracing your family back to its national origins is, at this stage, an exercise in putting the cart before the horse. The primary task at hand is that of compiling an *American* genealogy of your family. Then, depending on your inclination and the feasibility of it as regards your particular line, you may or may not decide to go any further. In any event, a complete American genealogy of your family is a wonderfully satisfying project to work on and to see through. It is also something which you can then pass on to your descendants. Something which will mean far more than any heirloom.

As you tackle your American line you will come across various types of challenges and at the same time will expand your knowledge of history and geography, but most importantly, you will gain an increasing understanding of just who you are and where you came from. This in itself is no small achievement.

If you are able to trace yourself back to the original immigrants (both paternal and maternal), and fill in all the spaces in-between, then excellent—you have a complete American genealogy, and congratulations to you. If you are unable to do so (as will happen to many people), then by no means should you regard your project as a failure. No one can accomplish what is simply not possible. Some, for example, after having exhausted all possible sources, will find themselves five generations back from themselves with nowhere to go. If this turns out to be the case with you, then your genealogy is complete in another sense.

It is complete in the sense that it represents all the information that is available and is then a solid building block for the generations which will follow you. In keeping your records, it is important to bear in mind the people of the twenty-first century who will be tracing their family line through you.

If you have already done some genealogical research, then you already know what a rewarding experience it can be; if you have yet to begin,* then some pleasant surprises are in

* Before you begin, be advised that the chapters in this book are arranged to treat subjects in the order that most people come to them in the normal course of their research. However, for many reasons which we will point out in the following chapters, every-

store. Either way, you have much to look forward to. Much could be written, indeed much has been written, about the unique joys of "ancestor hunting," but since you are soon to realize these joys first-hand, we need not touch on them here except to say that genealogy has been likened to a gigantic jigsaw puzzle—a jigsaw puzzle in which you yourself are one of the pieces. It is that, certainly, but at the same time it is bigger than that. It is a puzzle with life breathed into it. Life and, yes, excitement. It is nothing less than a hunt with all of the elements of a hunt. A hunt in which you must use your ingenuity and perseverance. A hunt which may ultimately lead you halfway around the world on paper or in actuality, and yet, almost paradoxically, back to yourself and a greater realization of your own place in the finely woven fabric of the history of mankind.

---

one's search is different and unique. Don't feel that you *must* follow any particular research pattern in order to succeed. What is very efficient for someone else may not fit your needs. After reading this book through once, just follow the dictates of your common sense as regards your own particular search. The book was written such that the various chapters are largely independent of each other and can be used in any order.

2

HOW TO ORGANIZE YOUR FINDINGS

Arthur S. Wortman

As we've said, there will be many intangible results of your research. But what of the other results? In other words, what will you have to *show* for your efforts?

George Olin Zabriskie, the author of *Climbing Our Family Tree Systematically,* discusses this matter of genealogical end products and remarks that:

> Genealogical information, no matter how extensive or scanty, how factual or faulty, how replete or sparse with enrichment material, is of no value slumberingly at rest in our work papers. In terms of real accomplishment we might just as well left it in its original source records. To locate and gather this information and then fail to put it to work in our permanent family records is like planning to build a new house, but stopping all action after assembling all necessary plans and materials.

As Mr. Zabriskie so succinctly points out, in genealogy just as in any other endeavor, an end product or goal is essential.

Your end product can take several different forms, from publishing a book to organizing an integrated collection of files.† But one of the most popular fruits of genealogical labor

† At this point we should mention an additional reward that can result from your interest in genealogy—a family organization. Family organizations can be initiated by any enthusiastic and dedicated genealogist who wishes to bring kinsmen bearing his family

Five Generation
PEDIGREE CHART

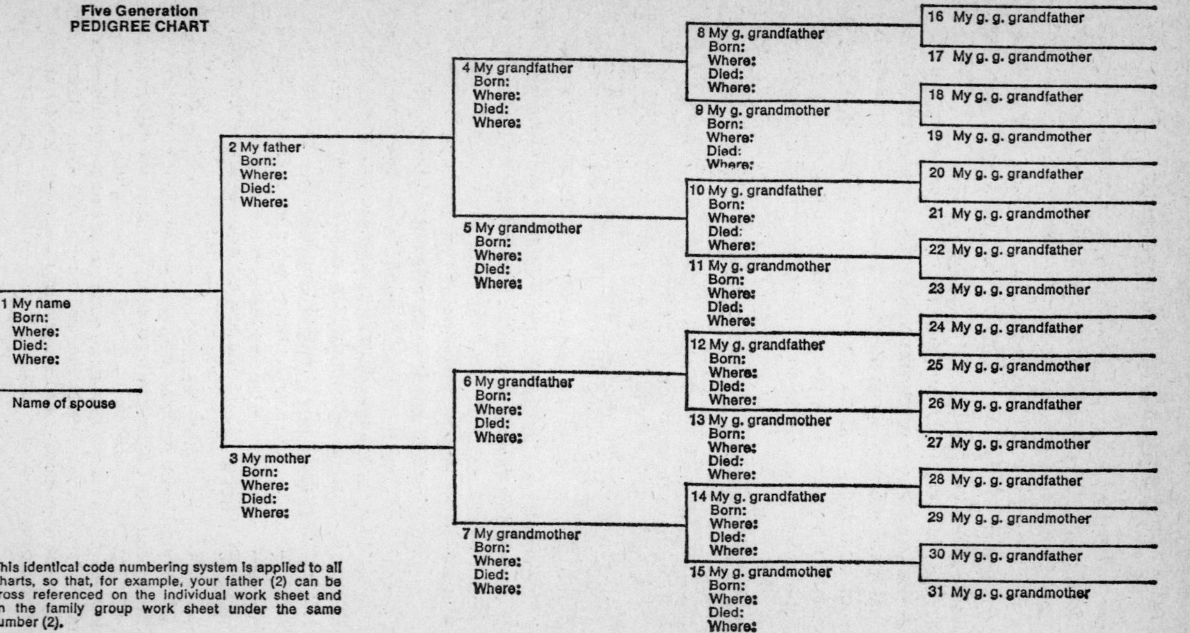

This identical code numbering system is applied to all charts, so that, for example, your father (2) can be cross referenced on the individual work sheet and on the family group work sheet under the same number (2).

is the *pedigree chart.* A pedigree is simply a recorded line of descent, and derives from two Latin words, *pes,* a foot, and *grus,* a crane. The reason for this is that the lines showing descent in early genealogies resembled a crane's foot. It was a well-known symbol and came to be synonymous with the study of genealogy itself.

A typical five-generation pedigree chart is shown on the opposite page, and it is recommended that, regardless of the genealogical end product you desire, you use such a chart as one of your work papers. Remember that it is just a work paper and that the final version may go back as far as ten generations or more. For a start, however, this chart takes you back five generations—to your great-great-grandparents, or, roughly, to the mid-1800s. Ideally, you should not fill it in at all until all sixteen necessary family group sheets have been completed and verified. Some, though, may find it useful to fill in the pedigree chart as they go along, either as a measure of progress or as an aid to help them visualize the overall picture of relationships. If you should decide to do this, bear in mind that you may very well have to make changes later on as new evidence comes to light. For this reason, it is best to write lightly in pencil on the pedigree chart during the research stage.

The next element to consider in your record keeping is the *coding system.* This is the thread which runs through and ties together all of your records. Looking at the pedigree chart, you'll notice that each individual has a unique numerical designation. All materials pertaining to any individual and his family are filed under that number which we will call the *code number.* Traditionally, in American genealogies the immigrant

---

name closer together for the purpose of maintaining family unity and working collectively to complete the history of your ancestors. This can be by far one of the most effective and productive means of compiling family records, with the added benefit of renewing old friendships and beginning new ones. To start the organization all you have to do is draw up a proposed constitution, stating the objectives of the organization, membership rules, and plans for family meetings; next, you can mail copies of these bylaws to everyone in your family, and from there, your genealogical adventure blossoms.

ancestor is considered to be a member of the first generation, his son a member of the second generation and so on. However, since most people who are just beginning their genealogical research are not yet quite sure of exactly how many generations have elapsed since the arrival of their particular immigrant ancestors, it is more useful and convenient to consider the person compiling the genealogy as a member of the first generation. Accordingly, the code number of you, the genealogist, is 1. The genealogist's father and mother are of the second generation, and are accordingly assigned the next two numbers in logical sequence, with the male head of household always given an even number and the female always given an odd number. Thus, your father is assigned the code number 2, and your mother, 3. This numbering system continues for each succeeding generation, always starting with the male head of household in your paternal line. Consequently, your father's father (your paternal grandfather) is assigned the next sequential number, 4, your father's mother (your paternal grandmother) is 5, your mother's father (your maternal grandfather) is 6, your mother's mother (your maternal grandmother) is 7, and so on. This need not get confusing if you remember to use the five-generation pedigree chart on page 8 as a "road map" for the first five generations.

Now let's take a look at the basic tools you will use, the *individual work sheets* and the *family group work sheets.* You can draw them up yourself or purchase them preprinted. There are minor variations among those which are sold, but generally they will be the same as those depicted on pages 11 and 12. The best way to keep these sheets is in a three-ring binder. This permits not only ease in filing, but also portability. On your trips to the library, courthouse, or other genealogical "hunting grounds," you'll certainly want to take these papers with you. We recommend that the family group work sheets and the individual work sheets be separated (perhaps by a tab), and filed, of course, in numerical order by code number.

The actual filling out of these sheets is self-explanatory, so only two points need to be mentioned here. Firstly, the family

INDIVIDUAL WORK SHEET

Code Number	

NAME in full: ______________________

BIRTH date: ______________________
place: ______________________

OCCUPATION(S): ______________________

MILITARY SERVICE: ______________________

DEATH date: ______________________

BURIAL date: ______________________
place: ______________________

MARRIAGE date: ______________________
place: ______________________

SPOUSE's name in full: ______________________
code number: ______________________

FATHER's name in full: ______________________
code number: ______________________

MOTHER's name in full: ______________________
code number: ______________________

RESIDENCES:

Town	County	State	Dates

ADDITIONAL BIOGRAPHICAL DATA (baptism, religious affiliation, etc.):

____

REFERENCES AND SOURCES USED FOR RESEARCH AND VERIFICATION (birth, date, and marriage certificates, wills, censuses, Bibles, etc.):

group work sheets are filed in numerical order by the code numbers of the heads of household, so the number sequence will be 1, 2, 4, 6, 8, 10, 12, etc., while the number sequence for the individual work sheets will be 1, 2, 3, 4, 5, 6, 7, 8,

FAMILY GROUP WORK SHEET

CODE NUMBER OF HEAD OF FAMILY

HUSBAND's full name (HEAD OF FAMILY):______

Places and dates of residences prior to marriage:______

______

______

WIFE's full maiden name:______

Wife's code number:______

Places and dates of residences prior to marriage:______

______

______

MARRIAGE date and place:______

CHILDREN

Name in full	Date and place of birth	Death date	Married to

FAMILY RESIDENCES

Town	County	States	Dates

MISCELLANEOUS DATA

______

REFERENCES AND SOURCES USED FOR RESEARCH AND VERIFICATION

etc. (Remember that *every* person shown on your pedigree chart has a corresponding individual work sheet, but only the genealogist and heads of families have corresponding family group sheets identified with their code numbers.) Secondly, the need for absolute accuracy cannot be overemphasized. These work sheets are your building blocks for the entire project. If an error is made here, it can only be repeated and compounded elsewhere.

To illustrate how the filing system works, let's consider some examples. If you want to find or enter information about your father, you would look under the family group work sheet filed under his code number (2). In addition, you would look at the individual work sheet marked 2, and the folder or envelope in your miscellaneous file (discussed below) bearing the number 2. The names of your father's brothers and sisters would be found on the family group sheet of his father (number 4). As another example, let's arbitrarily pick an individual whose code number is 16. Since 16 is an even number, we know immediately that the individual is a man. The pedigree chart tells us that he is in the fifth generation, paternal line. His name, birthplace, birthdate, death date, place of death, and the same information on his wife, all appear on the pedigree chart. Also, there will be a family group work sheet numbered 16, which lists his wife, children, residences, and other pertinent information. The individual work sheet numbered 16 lists still more information, and the miscellaneous file folder numbered 16 yields originals or copies of birth and death certificates, his marriage license, military records, photographs, and similar items.

We mentioned the *miscellaneous file* before, and, as you've probably gathered, this file can play as large or as small a part in your research as you want it to. To set it up, we suggest that you use a box, desk drawer, large folder, or any container large enough to file various sizes and types of data. While, for example, copies of any legal documents that you may be able to obtain are too bulky to place in your three-ring binder, they can easily be stored in this miscellaneous file. As soon as possible, attach the proper code number to that document. Photographs, old letters written by or about the individual, wills, all of these are things which you would want to put in the miscellaneous file under the appropriate code number. The point to be emphasized here is that almost all of the information you obtain about a family member will be of value at sometime, even if you cannot immediately put it on one of your work sheets. If you have no miscellaneous file, you'll soon find that you've mislaid bits of information or that you've simply forgotten them. Don't try to stretch your memory—keep your miscellaneous file in good shape and arrange it by code number in order to keep all records arranged and filed in a congruous manner.

A fairly common thing at libraries and courthouses is the sight of a genealogist, unversed in efficient filing methods, vainly trying to match scraps of paper from a pile, or painstakingly searching through his voluminous notes to try to find a simple birthdate. It is to help you avoid this confusion that this chapter was written. You are now familiar with all of the records-keeping aspects of genealogy that you need to know. You'll find as you go along that the system outlined above is wonderfully efficient and will save you much valuable time. So, with paperwork out of the way, let's begin the hunt!

3

HISTORY FOR GENEALOGISTS

William A. Roskey

All genealogical searches are alike, yet, at the same time, they are all different. Your ancestral background is, after all, yours and no one else's. No one can predict exactly where your search will take you, nor in what sequence, nor even how long it will take. There are many guides and general directions and procedures to make the trip easier, but no explicit method that will work with equal efficiency for everyone. In your particular case, for example, you may find it advantageous to consult the census records of the National Archives immediately after amassing names, dates, and places from the records you already have available around your house. Others, beginning with considerably less information, may find their next logical move to be a trip to the local courthouse.[1] No, your search is yours and yours alone, and it is impossible to say precisely when and where it will lead you.

Far from being a discouraging aspect of genealogy, this planning of your strategy, or drawing your own "roadmap," is one of the points which makes genealogy so appealing and attractive to so many people. We all like a certain amount of problem solving in our relaxation (whether it's choosing which move to make in a game of cards or doing a crossword puzzle), and a genealogical puzzle has the added bonus of being a *personalized* puzzle.

This chapter is devoted to still another bonus of genea-

[1] Of course, everyone's *first* stop is their own household (see Chapter 4), but after that initial phase, many divergent courses are open, depending on your own records.

logical research. When we begin to see our own forebears moving through the pages of American history, then the exciting story of our nation lives for us as it has never lived before. Antietam, Gettysburg, the Gold Rush, the Oregon Trail, Valley Forge—these names take on new meaning for us when we find that people whose blood now flows in our veins lived them.

Although, as we have said, no one can predict where your search will lead you, it is a certainty that history will play a large part in it. A knowledge of history is not only useful to, but in most cases, indispensable to the genealogist. Let us consider a typical example to illustrate the point. Imagine that your grandfather has told you that your ancestors came from Ireland because of the potato famine. Where does that bit of information lead us? Directly to the history books. There we find that the potato famine was in 1845, and that during that year and the four years following it, nearly a million Irish went to America. Thus, not only is your search for the arrival date of your immigrant ancestor narrowed, but you will probably read on to find out exactly what happened over there and how it came about that nearly a million people found it necessary to leave their homeland. You're learning history. Then you'll naturally want to find out what these people did when they arrived here. You'll find that the Irish immigrants were mostly country folk, small farmers, and laborers, and that once in America they tended to congregate in cities on the Eastern seaboard. We could pursue and amplify this example much further (such as learning how the Homestead Act and its ramifications fit in, or the profound changes wrought by such things as the Industrial Revolution and the Civil War), but you'll soon find on your own that the study of genealogy and the study of history are finely interwoven. Much has been written about this relationship; indeed, genealogy is often called "the handmaid of history." At one time, the two disciplines were virtually indistinguishable. Dr. Lester J. Cappon, director of the Institute of Early American History and Culture at Williamsburg (Virginia), has remarked that even a century ago "there was no thought of separating historical and genealogical activities." As you learn more about your own family and the events which shaped it, you'll also, unavoidably, be learning a good deal of history. For many, this is one of the most gratifying and interesting aspects of the whole exercise.

In fact, refreshing your memory on certain historical points before you even begin your search can save you countless hours in addition to making you aware of other avenues of inquiry. It will also help you to guard against misleading information and to better interpret your findings. It is toward these ends that this chapter is devoted.

Firstly, a common occurrence which almost never fails to confuse the novice genealogist is the practice of "double dating." In many early colonial American records, you will find entries like "12 February 1732/33," or "14 January 1701/02." The explanation for this seemingly strange practice is to be found, once again, in the history books. The various calendars in use prior to 46 B.C. were woefully inaccurate. It was in this year that Julius Caesar instituted a new (the Julian) calendar, which brought together lunar and solar time. Caesar determined that the solar year was 365 days and 6 hours, so his calendar made provisions for an extra day to be added every four years. But Caesar's calculations were off by 11 minutes and 14 seconds. Consequently, over the centuries, solar and lunar time began to drift apart again. By the year 1582, the deviation amounted to ten days. It was in this year that Pope Gregory XIII reformed the calendar. Firstly, he eliminated the ten-day discrepancy by directing that 4 October 1582 be followed by 15 October. Secondly; since the Julian error of 11 minutes and 14 seconds amounted to three days every 400 years, he further directed that those three days be dropped from the calendar by not observing any year which ended with two zeros as a leap year, unless the first two digits were divisible by four. Therefore, the years 1700, 1800, and 1900 were not leap years. But the year 1600 was, as will be the year 2000. By these simple expedients, Gregory once again brought lunar and solar time together. Now we get to the crux of the matter as regards early American records.

Not all countries accepted the Gregorian calendar at the same time. England and her colonies, in fact, waited until

1752 before embracing the new calendar. By that time, of course, the difference was eleven days. The eleven days were duly dropped from the calendar by the direction of Parliament that the day following 2 September 1752 would be 14 September. Many people at the time also added eleven days to their birthdates so that they might celebrate the exact anniversary. This explains why, for example, original records indicate that George Washington was born on 11 February, but that after 1752, his birthdate has always been considered to be 22 February. At this point, we must regretfully throw one last fly into the ointment. The original records indicate that George Washington was born not only on 11 February, but on 11 February *1731*. We recognize Washington's birthdate as 22 February *1732*. Now, we have already accounted for the eleven-day discrepancy. What about this business of an extra year?

For a long time, England and her colonies had been in the habit of observing two separate New Year's Days. The government and civil authorities considered 25 March to be New Year's Day, and the people at large considered 1 January to be the beginning of the new year. To return to the example of Washington's birthday, as far as the English government was concerned at the time, the year 1732 was still more than a month away. Needless to say, there was quite a bit of confusion. In an attempt to clarify things, many people took to using *both* years in their notations. For example, you will find dates similar to Washington's birthday written 1731/32. Or, you may find the same information expressed as 1731 O.S. (old style), or 1732 N.S. (new style). At any rate, along with reconciling solar and lunar time in 1752, the English government also officially recognized 1 January as New Year's Day. Therefore, you should only encounter double dating of years in or prior to that year. For the reasons given above, you will only encounter double dating of dates (e.g. 1/12 February, 3/14 March) in the months January, February, and March in or prior to 1752.

Equipped with the above information, you are already able to cope with one facet of genealogical research which has mystified and frustrated many a beginner. Now let us consider another problem area.

We all know that New Amsterdam is now New York City, and that Idlewilde Airport is now John F. Kennedy International Airport. But between these two name changes is a span of no less than three centuries with a myriad of other name changes, most of which are not nearly as familiar to the average person (nor to the average historian, for that matter) as our two examples. During that time numerous towns and geographical landmarks changed their names; many, more than once. States were carved from territories or from other states, and many counties, in turn, were carved from older counties. From time to time, states have changed their boundaries, counties have changed their boundaries, and growing cities have absorbed their suburbs. Some communities, as, for example, some mining towns, have simply ceased to exist altogether. Oftentimes genealogists have been unable to locate valuable information because they were unaware of the history of geography. We are by no means suggesting that the genealogist sit down and attempt to memorize the countless name and boundary changes of our nation's history. This is an impossible task anyway. It is simply enough to know and remind yourself that these things have occurred, and to know where to look for the pertinent information.

The definitive reference book on this subject is *The Handy Book for Genealogists,* edited by George B. Everton, Sr. This is an extremely helpful work for both amateur and professional genealogists alike, and probably the best way to illustrate its usefulness is to mention two of the hypothetical cases Mr. Everton gives in his instructions on how to use the book.

In the first example, we wish to find records on a man who, tradition[2] holds, was born in Missouri in 1811. But after checking the "Handy Book," we find that Missouri did not become a territory until 1812, and that from 1805 until 1812,

[2] At this point it is well to mention that genealogists should view all family traditions with extreme circumspection, and as facts which must always be verified. But even if inaccurate, many times they provide valuable clues.

it was part of Louisiana Territory. Therefore, we would begin our search for this particular man in the Louisiana records. Without knowing this bit of geographical history, one might well check the Missouri records, and failing to find the desired information, give up.

In the second hypothetical case, we have an ancestor who was one of the first settlers at Key West, Florida. We know that he arrived there in 1822 and died in 1823. Naturally, one very logical first step is to seek him out in the county records.[3] Key West is the seat of Monroe County, but we find that none of the records there help. Industriously, we check the records of six or eight neighboring counties, but still come up with nothing. Now, if in the beginning, we had consulted the "Handy Book," we would have learned that Monroe County was formed from St. Johns County in 1824, one year after the death of our progenitor. The "Handy Book" also informs us that St. Augustine (375 miles away from Key West) is the seat of St. Johns County. We then go there and find exactly what we want. For problems such as these, Mr. Everton's book is a time saver of the highest order. In addition, he includes helpful "check lists" of genealogical sources in each state, excellent bibliographies, and discussions of the availability of records in other countries as well.

We have examined how calendar changes and geographical place name and boundary changes can present stumbling blocks. Now let us consider another even more esoteric change—the change in language usage over the years (with particular emphasis on the meaning of words). As we begin to delve into old records such as letters, diaries, and wills, we will come across many familiar words, often assume we know their meanings, incorporate the information into our notes, and go on. Genealogically speaking, this can be extremely dangerous. This is because one or both of two unfortunate things are apt to happen. Firstly, we may overlook much interesting information, and, secondly, we may actually make mistakes and record incorrect information into our notes.

[3] County courthouses are veritable treasure troves for the genealogist and are discussed in detail in Chapter 6.

As a quick example of the first instance, let us assume that we have uncovered some eighteenth century record which says that one of our ancestors was transported to Virginia on board the ship *Forward Galley* on 18 June 1743. Now stop. Don't just write down that the man came over, or sailed, or arrived on the *Forward Galley*. The records says that he was *transported*. To us, of course, as twentieth century Americans, the word denotes carrying or conveying; to eighteenth century Americans, in this context, it meant something entirely different. It meant banished, or, if you will, deported. Many people were deported from England to the colonies, but often for far less serious crimes than merit deportation today. There were no less than 150 capital crimes in England for which a man might be transported. Of course, there were the expected offenses of murder, arson, treason, and the like, but there were also lesser ones such as maiming, stealing a cow, cutting down trees along an avenue, sending threatening letters, and standing mute when addressed by a legal official. Some convicts were even people of quality. One gentleman of high birth, for instance, was transported for stealing books out of a library. As a child, George Washington was taught to read and write by a transported convict who had been a schoolmaster. Especially in the countryside, the crimes which resulted in transportation were often very petty. One man was transported for stealing a silver shoebuckle. Another was sent to America and indentured for seven years for the theft of a chicken. It can readily be seen that, if you had not been familiar with this historical meaning of a word, you would have then missed out on the circumstances surrounding your ancestor's trip to America. In this particular case, as in many others, knowledge of a word will further increase the intensity of your genealogical and historical curiosity. For, naturally enough, you will not now rest until you find out *which* crime your ancestor was transported for.

As we have said, the second and more serious consequence by far of ignorance of language usage changes is the possibility of misinterpreting your findings. Particularly in the field of genealogy, a mistake is much more serious than an omission. A mistake will lead you down wrong trails and can waste months, even years, of your research time. An omission ends there, and at least does no harm.

The greatest cause of this second type of error is, paradoxically enough, problems with precisely the words that we use most often—brother, sister, cousin, nephew, even the title Mrs. has changed in usage through the years.

Whenever we see familiar words in old records, we must always remind ourselves that what we know are the *twentieth century meanings* of these words, and not necessarily the seventeenth, eighteenth, and nineteenth century meanings. Presented below are some of the more frequent problem words and their colonial meanings.

brother: one's own brother, but *also* often used to designate one's brother-in-law, stepbrother, husband of a sister-in-law, or "brother in the church." Sometimes even capriciously used for no apparent reason at all, except possibly to indicate good fellowship or friendship.

cousin: most often used to mean nephew or niece, but also could mean cousin in our modern sense of the word, *or* used to denote any family relationship (usually by blood, but sometimes others as well) with the exceptions, of course, of mother, father, son, daughter, brother, and sister.

freeman*: literally, a "free man," i.e., one who held the full rights of a citizen. A freeman could vote and enter into business agreements; an indentured servant could not.

gentleman*: a man of "gentle birth" (descendancy from an aristocratic family) whose income was obtained by the rental of his lands. Thus, a gentleman was a member of the *landed gentry*. If the son of an aristocratic family left home and took up a trade, he lost the title of "gentleman." If he left home but continued to live from rental or took up a respected profession such as law or the ministry, he retained the title.

* Terms of social position, these are actually ranks in the colonial social hierarchy, which ran, from the top to the bottom of the scale, thus: gentleman, goodman, freeman, and indentured servant.

goodman*: a respected and substantial member of the community who ranked below a gentleman, but above a freeman on the social scale.

goodwife*: the spouse of a goodman. The title was often shortened to "goody," and you will see references to women like "Goody Smith," or "Goody Jones." Remember that this is not a name, but the shortened version of a title.

indentured servant*: a person who had voluntarily (or involuntarily, as in the case of transportees) bound himself to work for someone for a fixed number of years, typically from four to seven, in exchange for passage to the New World. At the bottom of the social scale, the indentured servant had few rights, but many, many people chose this way of life in order to emigrate. For anyone who lacked the fare or a skill to support himself once he got here, it was the only way open. And, of course, once he had served the period of indenture, the servant became a freeman. It is interesting to note that the first black people to be brought to America were technically considered to be indentured servants, but the major difference here was that in most cases their indenture lacked a terminal date.

in-law: in addition to its modern meaning colonists also used the term to indicate *any* familial relationship which came about through marriage. Thus, a man's mother-in-law might either be his wife's mother or his own stepmother. His daughter-in-law might either be his son's wife or his own stepdaughter.

Junior, Senior, III, etc.: terms which *do not* necessarily mean a father-son relationship. They were used solely to differentiate between contemporaries with the same name to avoid confusion. David Smith, for example, might have a cousin or nephew named David Smith. The family would simply refer to the oldest of the two as David, Sr., and the younger as David, Jr. Many times, the juniors and seniors are not even related at all. In numerous small communities, there might be three or four men all with the same name and all unrelated. The communities simply named the men, according to age, as senior, junior, III, and IV. If John Jones,

Sr. died, John Jones, Jr. became John Jones, Sr., III became junior, and so on. If John Jones, Jr. died, III would become junior, and IV would become III. The same thing happened if any of these men moved out of the community; the remaining men would change their designations appropriately. These were not permanent designations, but temporary devices for the convenience of early American families and the small colonial community.

Mister: a prefix which could only be attached to the names of "gentlemen" (in the strict meaning of the word as described above), to the names of members of the clergy, or the names of those who held high civil office.

Mrs: mistress; the feminine equivalent of "mister," it was used in exactly the same way—to denote social position. It *was not* an indication of marital status, but of social status. Married and unmarried women alike carried the title.

nephew: usage generally the same as today. However, in very old records, can also mean the daughter of one's brother or sister. Again, in old records, but even more infrequently, the word was used to mean precisely what the old Middle English word (nevew) it derives from meant—grandson or granddaughter.

now wife (also present wife): term found exclusively in wills. It does not imply that there had been a previous wife. It was merely a safeguard that, in the event a man's wife died and he took another wife, the second wife would not be able to claim more than he intended.

sister: had exactly the same variations in meaning as brother (see above).

Lastly, let us consider the words *father, mother, son,* and *daughter*. Even today, we are not precise when we speak of familial relationships. We often speak of our mother-in-laws as our mothers, or of our stepchildren as our children. It is perfectly normal for a man to write of his daughter-in-law as "my daughter," or for him to speak of his adopted son as "my son." There is really no need to be precise in our day-to-day affairs about these things; indeed, if we were always meticulous about these relationships, we could conceivably even offend those that we love. The people who have lived before us were no different in this respect, and this is something that the genealogist must always bear in mind—this, and the actual change in word usage itself. Rarely, if ever, in genealogical research will we come across anything which is "obvious," but, equipped with a little bit of historical preparation, rarely should we come across items which are unfathomable either.

We have covered some specific historical points that the genealogist will run into. But he'll also find a general knowledge of American history useful. It would be far too ambitious an undertaking to attempt to write a history of the United States within the confines of this chapter, but we can take a brief look at the aspect of our history which fascinates genealogists most—immigration. As we have said in the Introduction, some people will wish to trace themselves back further than their immigrant ancestors; some will not. But, in any event, everyone's first goal should be to complete an American genealogy of their families. This means going from yourself back to your immigrant ancestor, the man in your family who first set foot on American soil. Now what about these immigrants?

Will Rogers, in poking gentle fun at those who take perhaps an inordinate amount of pride in their ancestry, used to remark that *his* ancestors (he was part Cherokee) were at the dock to meet the *Mayflower*. Figuratively, of course, he was right, and this serves to underscore the fact that every American either is an immigrant or has descended from immigrants, with the possible exception of the American Indians (*possible* exception because many anthropologists believe that the Indians themselves were immigrants). The story of American immigration is the story of a fabulous odyssey of an estimated seventy million people of many different backgrounds and nationalities. It is the story of their hopes, their fears, their aspirations: it is the story of America itself. Oscar Handlin, the noted historian, best expressed it when he said, "Once I thought to write a history of the immigrants in America. Then I discovered that the immigrants *were* American history." No single volume could possibly relate their magnificent story in all its breadth and scope, and the volume you now hold in your hands is no exception. However, there is much to be gained from a broad overview.

The first immigrants were the English, who were to lead all other nationalities in immigration until the first half of the nineteenth century, when Irish and German immigrants began to arrive in large numbers. Early English immigrants consisted, basically, of two different groups who settled in two different places: the Puritans in Massachusetts and the Cavaliers in Virginia.

Tradition holds that the early colonists were religious refugees from a dictatorial and unyielding monarchy which refused to acknowledge their basic religious rights. This tradition is right and wrong at the same time, for though most colonists were Protestants fleeing the conformity of England's state church, their flight arose from a multiplicity of issues touching on several important matters besides religion.

Beginning with Martin Luther in 1517, the Protestant Reformation experienced a rapid development and wide appeal throughout much of Europe and England. Preaching a doctrine of salvation through individual conscience rather than sacerdotalism, various Protestant sects had great political as well as religious significance.

In England, the Reformation was an important aspect of the politics of the monarchy. In this case, Henry VII appeared to embrace it in his attempts to divorce his wife and take a new queen: he instituted a new church which, though seemingly opposed to Catholicism, was really only slightly different, mostly in its organization. Throughout the mid-sixteenth century, the English religion swayed back and forth, tending in some aspects toward Catholicism and in others toward Protestantism. By the end of the reign of Queen Elizabeth I, the religion of England had become quite moderate.

This moderation was very political in nature, for it attempted to put an end to the agitation of the Puritans, or English Protestants, who sought to "purify" the English Anglican Church of its Catholic tendencies. Elizabeth's efforts succeeded for a time, but by the early 1600s Puritanism was definitely in ascendancy in England.

At the same time the economy of Europe and England was experiencing a similar kind of disruptive development. New wealth, mostly silver and gold from Spanish colonies in the New World, was causing tremendous inflation. Prices on all goods were rising very fast, and the poor, laboring classes were suffering most from this condition. In England, with its population of seven million people divided into groups of nobles, gentry, yeomen, and laboring poor, the economic problems of the age touched most heavily on the king. His income was fixed by Parliamentary law, and as he was expected to finance his office and authority wholly from his own pocket, he soon felt the squeeze.

This situation focused attention on the House of Commons which was composed of the gentry, or large land-owners and merchants, who were prospering from the inflation. In the House of Commons, these Englishmen could exert considerable influence over the king by their power of the purse. Most galling, perhaps was their refusal to give the king the power to tax individuals. His royal finances thus remained dependent on his own ingenuity and ability to devise various levies and duties to meet his needs. Such levies ultimately reached deep into the pockets of the laboring class.

Concurrent to the rise of Puritanism in England and inflation in the world economy, the Industrial Revolution led directly to great unemployment, particularly among the rural laborers. These people were forced into idleness by government policies which had enclosed the previously open fields of England in order to create land suitable, not for farming, but for raising the great flocks of sheep necessary to support the English woolen industry. Pressed by rising inflation, without work, and often in opposition to the state religion, the laboring poor of England were, by the early 1600s, easily inclined to consider emigration; it was the only solution to an intolerable situation.

Almost simultaneously, there developed the government policy of mercantilism, which encouraged colonization as a means of developing and extending the economic base of the country. Mercantilism was carried on by the joint-stock venture company, a group of merchants who received authority from the king to organize, finance, and conduct various colonizing expeditions. It drew on the large group of dissatisfied English workers for the supply of the colonists necessary to effect the policy of mercantilism. Thus, a combination of political, economic, and religious factors influenced greatly the developments which gave rise to the English colonies in North America.

The Puritans saw the New World as an ideal location for their "experiment in constructive Protestantism." They settled in Massachusetts, and the history of their colony actually begins with Captain John Smith. In 1614, two London merchants hired him to conduct a whaling expedition off the American coast, and although unsuccessful in that, he did bring back a shipload of fish that paid for the voyage. More importantly, he brought back a tremendous enthusiasm that translated itself into a best-selling pamphlet entitled *A Description of New England.* John Smith's bright, optimistic reports on "the Paradise" of New England greatly interested the Puritans. So it was that when they chose a place of refuge from the increasing religious intolerance in England, that place was the northern coast of North America. And when James I greeted their petition with the question, "What profits may arise in the parts to which they intend to go?" the Puritans replied, "Fishing." "So God have my soul," James exclaimed, "tis an honest trade! 'Twas the Apostles' own calling." He granted royal sanction, and so began the voyage of the *Mayflower* and the subsequent colonization of New England. In America, they were able to dedicate themselves fully to practicing their beliefs, rather than criticizing and trying to reform the English church.

Most influential in this development was John Winthrop, the governor of the Massachusetts Bay Company, who actually established a virtually autonomous colonial government in Massachusetts in 1629. His community, centered around Boston, was, however, a bit too strict for some of his followers, most of whom were simple laborers and merchants rather than Puritans. The rigid, unyielding autocracy imposed by the Puritan minority in Massachusetts soon gave rise to a new migration, this one heading out of Massachusetts and into the Connecticut River Valley.

The Connecticut Colony was located at Hartford and later became loosely tied with the New Haven Colony on the coast. Governed by a Puritan elite which put more emphasis on the commercial aspects of Puritanism (the emphasis has subsequently been described as the *Protestant work ethic*), the colony encouraged rapid growth and generated a growing number of other settlements, mostly populated by non-Puritan English yeomen and merchants.

Later, a flood of immigrants to Virginia was a direct result of the English civil war. Like all wars, the underlying causes were complex, and had been woven into the fabric of the whole society many years before. As discussed previously, Parliament and the king had come to an impasse over the issue of taxation and royal finances, and seeing the opportunity, English Puritans joined the antimonarchial forces. King Charles I attempted to force loans from the recalcitrant gentry and commercial class. The gentry refused, and Charles became desperate for money. The war was finally precipitated when the famous Long Parliament, which convened on 3 November 1640, repudiated the King's concepts of absolutism and rule by Divine Right. The members of Parliament demanded greater freedom and religious tolerance. When hostilities broke out, the battle lines were drawn between the Royalists, who supported the king, and the Puritans, who supported Parliament.

The Royalists were recruited from the Cavaliers, who were, for the most part, wealthy landowners and Roman Catholics; the bulk of the Puritan forces were drawn mostly from the common people. While the war, or actually, series of wars, raged from 1642 to 1649, many people, Puritan and Royalist alike, left the country for the New World, but Cromwell's final victory over Charles I prompted a huge migration of Cavaliers to Virginia. After Charles was beheaded in 1649, and the Puritans were in firm control of Parliament, it was declared to be an act of high treason to recognize Charles II or to attempt to "restore" him to the throne. Viriginia appeared to be the only refuge for supporters of the monarch; they were certainly not welcome in Puritan New England. Also, in Virginia, the Cavaliers found a social and economic system which was already similar to that of the English gentry. Large tobacco plantations were the outgrowth of the earliest settlements, and, as time passed, these plantations took on the aura of the English estate. From its beginning, the Virginia Colony had a significant population of gentry. In most cases the colonial gentry was made up of the younger sons of the English landed families. Because of *primogeniture,* the legal doctrine of inheritance of the estate by the eldest son, these younger sons often found themselves without any financial support once they reached their majority. Thus, emigration to Virginia offered a real opportunity for employment and the important chance for achieving high social standing.

However, in some circles, Virginia gained an early and completely undeserved reputation as "land of death." So much so, that some prisoners in English jails, when given the choice of emigration to Virginia or death by hanging, chose the latter. In fact, many people came because they were forced to—vagrants, paupers, thieves, even prisoners of war were deported to America, where they would be out of the way of decent folk and could do no harm except to each other. So it may be seen that great numbers of immigrants were actually *driven* to the New World, driven because of political, economic, or religious reasons, or sometimes more directly, driven out by the law because they were considered to be undesirables.

The profit motive brought others. In any great migration (just as, for example, in our own westward expansion), there are always those who see the tremendous economic potential in a new land. Although visions of easy riches in gold or silver most often quickly evaporated, there were still the cod-rich waters of Massachusetts Bay, tobacco in the southern colonies, furs, and new ports for trade up and down the virgin coastline. These riches of the New World accrued most to the mercantilists, but there were riches of a different sort for the common man. Some wanted nothing more than their own land and a fresh start. This opportunity was open to virtually every man. Even if he had to become an indentured servant for a while, this was not such a bad bargain as it may seem. The indentured servant received free transportation to America, and at the end of his contract, which was typically for four years, he received his *freedom dues.* This payment was usually clothing, a gun, tools, some money, and sometimes as much as fifty acres of land. The indentured servant had often learned a useful trade as well.

In addition to the three main reasons for emigration (religious persecution, political oppression, and economic considerations), other less obvious, more personal, and historically unimportant motives have caused people to pack up and come to America: the end of a love affair, escape from altercations, the desire to be with friends who were going, or perhaps just an adventuresome spirit. These were some of the reasons. However, human motivations are nothing if not complex, and undoubtedly many came for reasons unknown even to themselves. Perhaps all they felt was a strange beckoning from a New Land which could not be denied.

In spite of all the dissimilarities in their backgrounds and reasons for coming, all early immigrants had one experience in common: a long, dangerous, and extremely unpleasant voyage across the Atlantic. In 1902, Henry F. Thompson read a paper before the Maryland Historical Society in Baltimore. Entitled *An Atlantic Voyage in the Seventeenth Century,* it gives an absorbing account of exactly what such a journey entailed.

> The vessels which were in use in the seventeenth century were small, when judged the ideas of sea-going ships of the present day, for there were few over two hundred tons, as an inspection of the few returns (which are extant) of the naval officers of the Patuxent and Potomac Rivers will show. Although a few ships were from three hundred to five hundred tons, the greater number of them were from one hundred and fifty to two hundred and fifty, and more were under than over two hundred.

They were broad in the bow, the forecastle and the poop were raised high above the main deck, the main-mast was placed in the middle of the ship, the foremast as near the bow as possible and the mizzen where the builder thought fit. The books on navigation and ship-building, all speak of top gallant masts and sails but in no one of the log-books is there any mention of a sail above the topsail, although, of course, they speak of making and taking in the sails as well as of sending down topmasts and yards. They were but slow sailers and although instances occur of as much as eight miles an hour being made, it was when there was a fair wind and plenty of it, and with a smooth sea, but at no time was that rate kept up for twenty-four hours. When the wind was ahead, but slow progress was made, for no ship could sail "close to the wind," and often four or five miles was all there was to show for a whole day, and there were even times when they were further from their destination at the end of twenty-four hours than they were at the beginning. Rather than keep on against a head wind they would "heave to" or "try" as they said in those days. The *Bristow* arrived in York River on 8th March, 1701, having left London on 22 October, and her Master writes "a more terrible passage has hardly been known by man. I have been on this coast near twelve weeks within forty or fifty leagues by all estimation." He had become separated from the fleet, for although the *Gloster* did not arrive until the day after the *Bristow*, the latter found on her arrival several vessels which left London with her, but which had been in port eight or nine weeks.

Indeed, there is nothing in which a voyage, two hundred years ago, differed more from one to-day, than in the great uncertainty as to the time which was to be spent in going from one port to the other.

When a passenger started from London, he could not say within many weeks, how long he was to be on board the ship which was to take him to Maryland or Virginia, for, of the eleven voyages of which we have the records, they were from forty-seven to one hundred and thirty-eight days from London to the Capes, and from thirty-two to one hundred and thirteen on their way home.

The same vessel varied from forty-seven days to one hundred and two days, in coming from London, and from thirty-two to fifty-two in returning home.

A ship would often be three or four weeks from London before she took her departure from the Lizard, detained in the Downs or some port by head winds or storms, and it must have been an inspiriting sight, after a storm, to see the numerous vessels getting under way from the Downs; for there would be hundreds of vessels starting out for all parts of the world, the vessels bound for the Chesapeake Bay often numbering forty or fifty, as the captain of one of them says, "We Virginians keeping together," the name Virginian being often applied to all vessels bound in the Capes.

When the fleet was clear of the land, they steered for the Azores, and one or more ships generally sighted Flores and Corves, the most westerly of the islands. Then they steered for Cape Henry, and deviated as little as possible from a straight course, for their latitude they could find every day at noon, by means of their quadrants, but their longitude they could only estimate by calculating the distance run the course steered, making allowances for currents, leeway or a heavy sea knocking them off their course. Notwithstanding this rather uncertain calculation they were not far out of the way when they began sounding to find out if they were near land.

Although a large fleet of fifty or sixty vessels might leave England, they soon became more or less scattered, although there were some vessels always in sight of each other, and frequently in calm weather there were visits between the officers and passengers of the different vessels, who dined or spent whole days, of which custom the following extract from the log-book of the *Johanna* gives an example: "Mr. Baker hoysted out his boat and came on board of us. We spared them some tobacco to pipe, for it was very scarce with them. About 5 oclocke they went aboard again: the master of her was sufficiently in drink before he went."

It may be supposed that the great uncertainty as to the duration of the voyage would have caused some trouble in providing sufficient food and water for so many persons, but the food was composed principally of bread or ship-biscuit, salt meat, peas and cheese, all which would keep well for many months, and therefore it was only the space required for enough food and water that gave any trouble, and when it is recollected that it would be necessary to carry food and water for one hundred persons (including passengers and crew) for a voyage lasting perhaps five months it is evident that the provisions which were necessary would occupy a great deal of space.

In a contract made with the owners of the ship *Nassau*, of five hundred tons, to carry one hundred and fifty or more passengers to Virginia, the following stipulations were made in regard to food. The passengers to have the same allowance of food as the sailors, that is to say: "they were to have their allowance of bread, butter and cheese weekly, and the rest of the provisions were to be distributed daily: each passenger, over six years of age, was to have seven pounds of bread every week, each mess of eight to have two pieces of pork (each piece to be two pounds) with pease five days in the week, and on the other two days four ponds of beef with pease each day, or four pounds of beef with a pudding, with pease for the two days, and in the case the kettle could not be boiled each passenger was to have one pound of cheese every day. Children under six years of age to have such allowance in flour, oatmeal, fruit, sugar and butter as the overseers of them shall judge fit."

There were in this ship one hundred and ninety-one passengers, of whom twenty-five were under twelve years of age, and although there were some of all ranks in life there seems to have been no difference made between them as to diet and lodging.

The ordinary price of a passage to Maryland or Virginia was six pounds, but for this large party the price was five pounds, for each person over twelve years of age, and half price for children under that age.

The ship *Johanna* was on her way from London to Virginia in March 1675, when the following incident occurred, viz.: "About 12 o'clock last night some of our people saw something walke in the shape of a dog and after that it was heard betwixt dex cry like a child and sometimes knocking without bord and the dog that belonged to ship run whineing up and down and crept in among the passengers I pray God dyliver us from all evil."

Nothing happened to them on the voyage, and they arrived in Virginia after a quick passage, and without any accident, but two years later on the same ship something happened which caused the death of two men, but what it was, is not very clear. "One of our servants was missing, judged he fell overboard and drowned: and another had his leg cut ofe, his other being cut ofe sometime before—they were boath Cap. Beales servnts."

If the vessels were long in crossing the ocean, they were also sometime in port, before they were ready to return home.

The *Constant Friendship* arrived in the Saint Mary's river on the 20th December 1671, and the next day, the Master went ashore and entered the ship at the Custom House. They lay there 10 days, landing passengers and goods, and then sailed for the Patuxent "to do some business there," and while there they buried a passenger, the 2nd mate, and one of the seamen. At the end of the week they sailed for the "Seavorne" which they reached at 2 a.m., sailing in boldly, "there being moonlight and fair weather." For two months and a half, they were delivering goods and taking in tobacco. Some of the English goods were consigned to different persons, and some were sold from the ship, payment being made in tobacco. The ship lay at anchor in the river, and the tobacco was brought off in shallops from the landings to which it had been rolled from the plantations. By the 25th March, they had on board about five hundred and fifty hogsheads, and they sailed for the Patuxent, where they took in more tobacco, and then went to St Mary's where by the end of April they finished their loading, having seven hundred and eight hogsheads on board, and cleared the ship, when they were ready to sail.

The ships generally spent three or four months in the rivers, delivering their goods and taking in tobacco, which was taken on freight, or obtained by "trucking" as it was called, that is to say, bartering the English goods for the tobacco, or sometimes the skins of wild animals, of which a goodly number were exported in the early days of the Colony. When the loading was finished, and the ship was cleared and ready for sea, they went to Lynnhaven Bay, where the fleet for England was made up, and received their sailing orders. One of the fleet was named as the Flag ship, and her commander was appointed Admiral with a certain authority over the Masters of other ships, subject of course to the orders of the Commander of the Men of War who conveyed the fleet off the coast or at times all the way to England. A Man of War lay in the Chesapeake, whose duty among other things was to convoy the ships 25 or 30 leagues off the coast, for there was great danger of an attack by Pirates who hovered about the coast, and sometimes ran into the bays and harbours to make a capture, but seldom, if ever, roamed over the ocean in search of their prey. The Governor of Virginia, at times, went out in the Man of War to see the fleet safely on their way, and when he arrived on board, most of the ships fired a salute, for they all had guns, and a gunner was a member of every ship's company as surely as a carpenter or sailmaker.

A "fleet" frequently numbered fifty vessels, or more and on the 31st July 1702 one hundred and forty vessels sailed out of the Capes convoyed by four Men of War. . . .

Even where there was war between Great Britain and some other country, there was not much danger of capture on the high seas, but when they got near the land the privateers, or "Capers," as Duch privateers were called, were cruising about, watching for the incoming ships, and sometimes capturing and carrying them off. One such incident is told in the log-book of the *Johanna*, under the date of July, 1676—"When Twart of Beachy Head saw severall shallops Frency Privateers come up with us and commanded our boat out and us by the lee but I would not being able to Deale with them: we saw them clap several Vessels aboard and plunder them and caryed two away at 10 o'clock in the night two came up with us together which command us to strick and by the lee which I would not they fired 3 gunnes at us but hitt us not the shot fell by the ships side, then they came close up and said they would clap us abord both together I bid them keep ofe or else we would fire att them we gott two of or guns upon the forecassell and poynted them aft at them for they intended to come aboard upon the quarter we could not bring a gun to beare upon them with [until?] we had don so: the french seeing us in preparation to defend ourselves bid us good night and left us after many bad words which passed between us. We fired not at them." The encounter with the privateers ended happily enough, nothing worse than an exchange of "bad words" having happened, but owing to the preparations for defence, one of the men on the *Johanna* lost his life, as the log-book tells in the following words: "Att 3 of Clock this morning the Carpenters mate being laid down to sleep upon the forehatch by the windlass and one of the guns upon the forecassel standing upon a pease and my mate goeing up on the for Cassel tooke holde of the mussell of the gun which oversett it it not being lashed Dumbled doune upon the deck and bruised the head of the Carpnters mate and broke his scull very much he dyed presently which was a very sad accident. We keept him until he was could and stiff and buryd him in the sea of thy South forland which I pray God have mercy upon his soule for he was suddenly taken out of this world. . . ."

There were other dangers that menaced the ships, even when they were thought to be past all the perils of the sea; and there is one more extract which tells of the end of the *Baltimore,* which had made many voyages to Maryland, and was considered a strong, well built ship. In 1673 she had made the passage home in very good time, and with the rest of the London Fleet had gone into Plymouth harbour—on the 18th September, all thinking, no doubt, that they would soon land their tobacco in London. They lay there for three days, and then started to go on to London but as all the ships could not get out in time a signal was made, for those that were outside to return. When the *Baltimore* got back the log-book says: "it was darke we run in behind the Island and ankored in 6 fad the wind ab S S E and blowed hard and rained we struck out topmasts and yards and rod about 2 hours fast but the wind blowing harder and harder we let go the sheet ankor and in vering away upon the best bower started the best vower ankor and nether that not the sheet ankor would take hold againe but we drove ashore upon the rockes about 3 ships lengths to the westward of milebay and being a high water and falling we presently sued and struck fast and bilged upon the rocks the next tide the water ranne over part of the gun deck: we saved about 60 hhds dry and all the ships materialls as guns cables ankors and rigging and sayles; and could not save the shipp although it wass indevoured by the plymouth men: but she stove all to peeses. . . .

I pray God send me better fortune the next voyage."

English immigration to America continues even to the present day. Only a few short years ago, the "Brain Drain," or immigration of British scientists and technicians, was the subject of much reportage. But, by the first half of the nineteenth century, England had ceased to be the *predominant* supplier of new settlers. At this point in history, Irish and German immigrants began to pour in. As with the English before them, their motivations were diverse and complex, but there were also general reasons. As for the Irish, it is estimated that nearly one million came in a five year period as a direct result of the potato famine (1845). Many Germans came because of the heavy suppression of liberal thought which came about as a national reaction against the reform ideas of the French Revolution. This suppression manifested itself in strict censorship of the press, of public meetings, and of schools and universities. The friction between the liberals and conservatives finally resulted in open hostilities in 1830, and again in 1848, with two unsuccessful revolutions. As is illustrated by the English civil wars prior to this, and the Russian Revolution nearly a century later, any internal upheaval in a nation produces its refugees, and these refugees in turn become immigrants, many of them, over the years, American immigrants.

In general, immigrants followed certain distinctive migration patterns once they landed, and the Germans and Irish are two good examples. The Irish, since they generally arrived dirt poor, in fact, had come precisely *because* they were poor, had no real option but to say where they had landed—in cities on the eastern seaboard, particularly in New York and Boston. The first and most essential order of business for an Irish immigrant was to get a job. This usually presented no problem, indeed, contractors actually waited at the docks to sign up Irish laborers as soon as they set foot on shore. But while the Irish could survive and did get an economic foothold, they had virtually no mobility.

The Germans, however, could afford to go about the business of settling at a more sedate pace. Unlike the Irish, the Germans left home not because of economic disaster, but for political or intellectual reasons, or simply because they wanted to better their lot. Consequently, they usually arrived with some savings, and a clear-cut destination: the rich farmlands of the Midwest. After the early German immigrants had staked out farms in Pennsylvania, New Jersey, and New York, the later German immigrants sought their homesteads in Illinois, Wisconsin, Ohio, and Minnesota.

In passing, the desire for a homestead as a motive for both immigration and migration cannot be underestimated. A great impetus was given to both movements on 20 May 1862 when the Homestead Act was signed into law by Abraham Lincoln. The law gave to "any person who is the head of a family, or who has arrived at the age of twenty-one years, and is a citizen of the United States, or *who shall have filed his declaration of intention to become such,*" the right to 160 acres of land for only a filing fee and the stipulation that he live on it for five years and make certain improvements.

The immigrants wrote letters (mostly enthusiastic) home, and these letters prompted still others to make the long, one-way journey across the Atlantic. Marcus Lee Hansen, in his comprehensive study, *The Atlantic Migration, 1607-1860,* reveals an interesting sidelight about the letters home.

> A persistent belief existed that letters were tampered with; that no communication derogatory to the country was allowed to leave; that to encourage immigration false letters of praise were concocted and signatures forged—a simple enough matter at a time when many of the senders, being illiterate, had to depend upon another's pen. To guard against interference and to prevent fraud, ingenious devices were adopted. Before departure it would be agreed that the emigrant's letters should be written upon a certain variety of stationery, or bear a device pricked by pins in the corner, or have the sealing wax applied in a place agreed upon, or a bent pin or small coin hidden in the wax. Occasionally a code would be adopted in which words did not mean exactly what they said. Thus a departing Irishman arranged that, if he advised his brother not to follow him without their dear grandmother, then, in view of the fact that the venerable dame had been dead thirty years, the advice should be interpreted as an adverse report.

The latter half of nineteenth century saw the Italians and those from the various eastern European countries supplant the Germans and the Irish as the numerical leaders of American immigration. Immigrants from Scandinavia as well began to arrive as the twentieth century approached. Their reasons were essentially identical to those of all the immigrant groups who preceded them. Whole books could be written on each immigrant group, from the first English settlers to those who followed nearly three hundred years later: the 5 million

Italians, the half million Greeks, the one and a quarter million Swedes, and all the others who had the courage to start a new life. But each group has its own story, its own heroes and villains, its own peculiar problems of adjustment. They are all different, yet finally, not so different. All of these immigrant groups have had to overcome prejudice and hardship. They have all made vast and important contributions to American culture and progress. In the agonizing and often heartbreaking business of building a new nation, they have all faced obstacles and triumphed—triumphed with quiet pride and dignity; they have all become Americans.

4

YOU AND YOUR FAMILY AS RESEARCH SOURCES

Ann I. Mahoney

Where do you begin to trace your genealogy? Start with yourself as the seed of your fruitful adventure. A "how-to" book on genealogy can give all genealogists basic guidelines and procedural steps to follow, but each genealogist's explorations will chart unique, individual paths leading to unique, individual destinations. Yet the starting point—the essential and initial step of the quest—is fundamental to all genealogists: begin with yourself, for you are the center of your universe.

You are an intriguing depository of genealogical data. The means and methods of exploring your past extend from you. Perhaps an analogy can best demonstrate just how logical this beginning is. If you decide to make a trip to the supermarket to purchase all the food you'd be needing for the coming week, certainly you'd start by looking in your own refrigerator, first, to see what you already have at hand. Nothing is more infuriating and wasteful than going to the store, buying a carton of milk, but returning home to discover you already had a whole carton of milk, and knowing it will go sour if you don't use it. You've wasted money, time, and effort for something you had in the first place.

Likewise; it would be just as futile and unnecessary to start your genealogical quest at any point other than with yourself. A false start can only lead to confusion and complications. If the foundation of your genealogy is weak, the structure of lives which you build upon it has little chance of standing on firm ground. Histories, genealogies, and biographies are each interrelated; histories of nations are founded on histories of families, which in turn are founded on histories of individual persons. The individual, obviously, is the root of every genealogy.

Thus, a systematic and productive genealogy—by its very nature—must begin with you, the individual. Whatever your motivation (seeking membership to an hereditary society, fulfilling religious obligations, or simply satisfying your own curiosity) and whatever your objective (a pedigree chart, a published genealogy, etc.), your efforts to trace your lineage should not only begin "at home," but should also follow a planned, logical sequence. You may at times be thrown off your charted course, but as long as you have a systematic plan (and everyone's plan will vary, depending upon what he already knows, what precisely he wishes to discover, and what sources he has available), your inquiries will inherently follow your directions.

Commence your genealogy by recording on paper all facts about yourself that are relevant to your inquiry. You might initially feel this is a waste of time and ask why should you record information about yourself when you just plain "know" it. There are two very sound reasons for this. First, getting into the habit of thoroughly recording all available information is essential to an accurate and valid genealogy. Genealogy is a documented account of family relationships based on oral and written records and on original and secondary evidence. If you approach the details of your own life with this in mind, your future research will be enriched. It takes a conscious effort to form the habits of a sound researcher. If you discover what questions to ask of yourself, you'll simultaneously be learning what questions to ask of others in your search.

Secondly, your genealogy will gain its fullest value if it is not only informative for you, but for your descendants as well. Say, for example, your name as recorded on your birth certificate was John Thomas Lane, but as the years went by, everyone called you Thomas Lane. By the time you were twenty-one, you dropped usage of your first name entirely and always referred to yourself as Thomas Lane and always signed your name Thomas Lane. If in your genealogical records you fail to note this spontaneous alteration, future generations will undoubtedly be confused as to the identities of John Thomas Lane and Thomas Lane. The more genealogical research you do, the more you will come to appreciate the necessity to clarify these small discrepancies, to your own benefit and that of others.

Interviewing yourself can be fun, for you inevitably know more about yourself than anyone else. One possible suggestion for documenting your data is to keep a record of the "bare essentials" (your full name, date and place of birth, and, if applicable, date and place of marriage) on a pedigree chart (see chapter two); for all additional facts, use an "individual work sheet" (also see chapter two). As you build onto your pedigree chart (starting with yourself [and your spouse], then with your parents [and your spouse's parents], then your parents' parents, etc.), you'll have an easy and quick reference to your lineage. But don't hesitate to jot down all the interesting tidbits of your own life and others on the individual work sheets. That is, in fact, what these sheets are for—expounding on the facts. The point to be made here is simply that a genealogy of nothing but names, dates, and places makes for extremely dull reading. Not until you can fill those statistics in—with personality traits, outstanding achievements, peculiar interests, etc.—are the numbers transformed into distinct characters.

You'll learn the most about yourself and about others by constantly asking and acting. Seek the answers to the traditional questions of "who, what, where, when, how, and why." Search through your own papers to locate the answers to these probes. Verification of the facts you've collected—whether about yourself or someone else—involves assembling, organizing, and analyzing documentation of the source data. Remember that evidence (either as testimony or records) of an event is not necessarily proof of that event.

Once you've exhausted your own supply of genealogical data, you should approach the closest relative about whom you need information or from whom you can clarify information about someone else. Of course, you should always make every effort to go directly to the person you wish to question, but if that person is no longer living or for some reason you are unable to contact that person, attempt to communicate with the person(s) most closely related to your subject. As stated earlier, the logical sequence is simply to fill in the facts about one generation at a time, starting with yourself and working backwards. Already you can see how each genealogist's quest, while commencing at the same point (with himself), will inevitably follow different courses.

If, for example, I need to learn the names of my maternal grandmother's brothers and sisters, I would go directly to my maternal grandmother; if, however, she were deceased, I would naturally have to explore other avenues of approach. Yet I would still attempt to gather these facts through direct interviews, telephone conversations, and/or written correspondence with other living relatives or friends, before consulting local vital statistics or similar records. As long as we're talking about a subject who could conceivably have lived during your own lifetime, the direct, personal approach is most efficient and most informative for your initial inquiry. Then, only after gathering the evidence in this manner, would you try to locate substantiating records. (How and where to find and use these innumerable records is explained in subsequent chapters of this book.)

Barring the most bizarre circumstances, only a fool would walk around the block to get to the house nextdoor; needless to say, it would be a waste of energy and time. Similarly, if members of any generations prior to yours (assuming that at this point you have already completed investigations at your own generation) are still living, seek your genealogical data directly from them, as opposed to first searching local records or approaching friends of your living relatives. Whenever feasible, arranging for an interview with, for example, your great-aunt, is the easiest and most efficient method of questioning an older relative. Inevitably, however, this is not always possible.

If the geographical distance is too great, a letter of inquiry is the second best approach. (People, particularly older people, are frequently inhibited by the telephone; in the other extreme, many older people tend to "ramble" on the telephone and the conversation is difficult to control.) Make your letter as succinct and clear as possible, both in its format and content. Briefly explain the motivations for your genealogical inquiry and then present your questions in a logical fashion, leaving plenty of space for the answers (a questionnaire form is usually the most effective and efficient). Don't ask irrelevant questions and never be vague in your questioning. The more precise your question, the more likely your answer will be specific. Try to limit the number of inquiries in any one letter.

Older people often find it difficult to write (many times because of physical handicaps), but will be even more hesitant to respond if they are overwhelmed by the length of your inquiries. Older people also frequently have visual problems and a double-spaced, typewritten letter is by far the easiest to read. As a tactful consideration that would indicate your earnest desire for a reply and your earnest attempt to make that response as easy as possible, enclose a self-addressed, stamped envelope. Generally, if you take the time to make a considerate and systematic approach in your letter, you will achieve the results you're looking for.

Regardless of the medium employed for communication, care should always be taken to treat your subject with diplomacy and discretion. In applying this rule of etiquette to personal interviews, arrange your meeting well in advance and whenever possible, supply your subject with a basic outline of the questions you intend to ask prior to the actual meeting. This will help alleviate any qualms your subject may have about the interview and can give him the chance to prepare for your inquiries. You yourself should come to the interview prepared to take notes. An oral interview has a number of advantages over written correspondence. Generally, it should not be too difficult to establish a relaxed and informal atmosphere. This, in turn, will stimulate spontaneous answers, so that the information you gather will likely be more complete and more interesting. In addition, the interview approach allows you to adapt or alter your line of questioning as the need arises. Finally, with an interview you are afforded the opportunity to return to questions about which you are uncertain for further clarification.

On the other hand, interviews can be tricky unless handled correctly; certain precautions should be taken. For starters, suppose that for some reason you're on unfriendly terms with your grandfather, whom you wish to interview. Your interest in his past may be the key to establishing friendlier grounds of communication, so a special effort should be made to explain your interest in genealogy. If, however, you know your grandfather would never agree to an interview with you, try an indirect approach: solicit the assistance of another relative or friend who could talk to your subject. Just remember that if this step is necessary (another instance that demonstrates how naturally each genealogist's course will vary depending upon his circumstances), keep in mind that the data collected is second-hand. And, of course, realize that if your grandfather says he doesn't want to talk with you next week, that does not necessarily mean he'll never talk with you. But once you've decided to do a genealogical study, try to interview your older relatives as soon as possible. If you're feeling lazy in this respect, you may regret it later, should your older relative die in the interim. Don't waste the sources you already have. It's a point to be taken seriously: act now and don't put off until tomorrow what you can do today.

Once an appointment has been made for the interview, select your questions wisely. If, for instance, you are aware of a "family scandal" and feel it may be a touchy subject, approach the issue with discretion. Explain to your subject your reasons for even touching on the point and impress upon him the necessity of uncovering any facts he may be able to supply. Should your subject still remain very reluctant to discuss the issue, do not press him too hard. Chances are you could bring the topic up at a future meeting or you might discover someone else who would be able to supply the facts.

Also take care to avoid what is referred to as "interviewer bias." Often the manner in which you word a question will determine just how your subject will respond. Avoid intimidating your subject or influencing his answers. Never start your questions with the phrase, "you do remember, don't you, . . .", for you are immediately putting your subject on the defensive. If you keep your questions as direct, objective, and simple as possible, you'll undoubtedly achieve the best results.

For example, if initially you want to ask your grandfather when his brother was born, don't ask, "Your brother Robert was born in September 1899, wasn't he?" This approach of supplying the answer to your own question tends to greatly influence your subject's answer. Most subjects want to please their interviewer, so that if your grandfather was actually quite uncertain about his brother's birthdate, he might simply agree with you to avoid any embarrassment and to avoid having to say "I don't know."

But you, as a genealogist, are seeking the most accurate evidence possible and if it turns out that your grandfather is actually uncertain about the fact, you should be aware of his uncertainty. If, instead, you had simply asked, "Do you know when your brother Robert was born?", you'd be getting much closer to the truth. In this case, your grandfather is freely allowed to express his uncertainty and either you and your grandfather, or you alone, can then check family or town records to get your answer. Even if your subject is unable to supply the answer to your question, it is highly probable that he will be able to direct you to the answer.

This brings up still another point to remember while interviewing older people. Everyone knows that with time your memory begins to play tricks with you. In particular, people over seventy frequently cannot recall what took place last week, but can instantly recall in detail an event that occurred forty years ago. Forgetfulness is a trait we all share to different degrees at one time or another, but few of us are forgetful about absolutely everything all of the time. Never assume that because your great-uncle Joe always forgets what day it is, he would be unable to help you in your search for genealogical data. I think you'll be pleasantly surprised at just how much an older relative or friend is capable of recalling. Also remember to continue to go back to questions which have been unanswered. While your great-uncle Joe may not recall a fact at one point in the conversation, he may remember it later on in the conversation, or he may remember it a week later. Often a simple, unrelated comment will set off a spontaneous recall just by chance (this is one of the benefits of holding an oral interview). In any case, you should do your best to prompt the answer, but without pressing too hard. If necessary, set up another interview and return to the question then. Additionally, never press the powers of your own memory too far—as stated earlier, keep your own accurate notes during the meeting. You'd be surprised at just how much you can forget after the lapse of an hour or a week.

Whether or not you have just one interview or several, let your subject know that your interest is sincere and that any additional information that your subject might be able to supply is truly appreciated. Always provide your subject with a means of getting in touch with you, whether by phone, written correspondence, or personal interview. Once you've made the effort to open the doors of communication with an older relative, keep the lines of communication open.

Whenever possible, arrange for a second interview. You may realize from the very beginning that you have too many questions for one sitting. While gathering too much information is generally better than too little, avoid making your interview unpleasantly long. Remember that older people tire quickly. Setting up two interviews allows you to assess your first interview for the general direction that your questions took and the effectiveness of those questions. Perhaps the results of your first interview will suggest a new line of approach, present new questions to probe, or give you an opportunity to elaborate on earlier questions. Once again you can see just how differently each genealogist's study will unfold; each genealogist's "next step" in research is inevitably his own, unique course, suited to and patterned after his own, unique inquiries.

The time between interviews can be well spent by checking into other possible leads or by verifying the information obtained from the interview. Note any discrepancies that may appear. While you may highly respect your subject's integrity, there is always room for error when recalling information; additionally, one source of data is not sufficient to make your evidence "fact." Your subject may himself be able to supply the necessary verification by showing you family records. Make your best effort to either obtain the original record or have copies of it made. You may discover, while reviewing your notes of the interview, that several anecdotes or reminiscences mentioned by your subject actually contains bits of information you need. While you have to be discrete in separating fact from myth, it's usually not an impossible task and leads taken from these stories can often prove to supply rewarding genealogical data.

Generally there is some element of truth in most "family traditions," but the alert genealogist needs to carefully decipher where fiction commences and fact terminates. Just about everyone wants to be associated with prestigious figures in our country's history, but not everyone in America could possibly be related, for instance, to George Washington. If family tradition has it that one of your ancestors was related to President Washington, and you've heard this story from several relatives, don't scoff at what you consider to be a highly implausible fact. Rather, take the time and effort to weed out the truth. More than likely there was some reason for the story to have evolved in the first place. Perhaps you'll discover that the ancestor in question was a soldier in one of Washington's units, was the maker of a carriage for the Washingtons, worked as a gardener on Washington's estate, or some equally fascinating bit of history. While your subject was certainly not deliberately lying, reminiscences of this nature—passed on orally from one generation to the next—tend to become grander and grander with time. In probing the origin of the family tradition you may uncover a fact that, while of less magnitude, is equally significant and equally intriguing.

Getting the facts—even those hidden in legend—is all part of the genealogist's task. Making you and your family your first research source involves turning evidence into fact by verifying the data you've collected (by phone conversations, by written correspondence, or preferably by oral interviews).

Family records are essential for proving the validity of your evidence. In early America one volume almost every family owned was the Bible. By tradition the head of the household usually recorded the vital statistics of his family members (birth, marriage, and death dates) in the family Bible. While today this custom is not nearly as frequently adhered to, one of your older relatives may have in his possession such a Bible. Often this source of data is the only available verification, if church or local records have been accidentally lost or destroyed. When other records are simply not available, Bible records, are in fact, accepted as reliable by most patriotic and hereditary societies. Note should be taken, however, to check the printing date of the Bible with the dates of family entries; in this fashion you can easily determine if some of the dates were recorded "after the fact," in which case you have to take into account a greater margin of error. Also check the handwriting, if it varies noticeably, in all probability the data was recorded as it occurred by each current household head. If, on the other hand, all entries were registered in the same handwriting, chances are great that a particular member of the family recorded all the vital facts about his ancestors that he could recall, and again the margin for error increases. Generally, however, entries in family Bibles are accurate and supply the researcher with invaluable information which should not be overlooked.

Diaries are another interesting source of genealogical data available from family members. A number of colonial diaries have been reprinted which supply valuable information not only to direct lineal descendants of a family, but to anyone interested in history. Any diaries found in your family should be carefully read. Even if a diary fails to provide any new information, it can often give you a keen insight into a particular ancestor's personality—an insight that you could not in all probability obtain from any other source. In addition, diary entries often provide clues to the political trends, social habits, and religious mores of the time—all fundamental to a better understanding of your subject. At its best, a diary can serve to verify evidence you already have or supply new evidence. Don't hesitate to rummage through an old box of books stored away in some relative's attic—you might be lucky and find a diary that no one knew about or that no one had thought significant.

Other possible records available from family sources include files of family papers (which could, for instance, contain earlier versions of a will or unrecorded deeds), high school or college diplomas, old passports, social security cards, military discharge papers, ledger books, photographs, samplers (often dated and often with the names of an entire family embroidered on it), quilts (these were often signed by the maker[s] and dated), old pieces of initialed silverware, or even old letters. As a portion of some ancestor's personal history, each of these genealogical sources is often capable of verifying information, presenting new information, or serving as a guide to other records.

Once you have exhausted your immediate family (and its bank of genealogical data) as a research source, you can try contacting far-removed relatives or persons with a similar name (you may discover relatives you didn't know existed) through correspondence or newspaper advertising. The *Hartford Times*, the *Genealogical Helper*, and the *Handbook of American Genealogy* are all publications which make correspondence between families of the same or different names possible. Family associations often print a magazine or newspaper which provides space for persons to make inquiries. This medium as an exchange of information among families is invaluable.

For centuries the ancient Egyptians, the Romans, and the Chinese used the histories of their own families for compiling their noble lineages. While most of us today have a much less illustrious scope in mind, anyone can compile his own lineage in a systematic and ultimately rewarding method. Genealogy is simultaneously a study of individual character, a study of family history, and a study of the history of a nation. As a genealogist you have the opportunity to watch and record the interplay of these three elements, each influencing and being influenced by the other. Your genealogical exploration, by simple logic and practicality, begins with yourself and with your immediate family. In your eagerness and enthusiasm to complete a pedigree chart or discover your heritage, don't let this most abundant store of genealogical data lie untouched. As your first step in compiling your own genealogy, take advantage of the resources available at hand. As emphasized throughout this chapter, after the initial starting point, each genealogist's quest will follow variant courses, specific to your unique motivation, family resources, and overall goal.

5

PRINTED SOURCES

AGRI Staff

For a great many, the first step after collecting and correlating information gathered from their own families will be a trip to the library. Americans have always made good use of their excellent free libraries, and it is almost a national tradition to begin any new home project with a visit to the local library. Regardless of how you decide to map out your research plans, visiting the library in the early stages is highly recommended, if for no other reason than just to find out what's there. Some people (few and far between, but nevertheless it happens) have discovered printed genealogies concerning their families on the shelves and were immediately able to tie themselves in, thereby saving countless hours. Of course, library resources differ widely, depending on such things as the size of the community, amount of financial support, and so on. Consequently, no one can tell you exactly what's in your library except your librarian. However, the following four bibliographies in this chapter have been included to serve as a guide of what to look for.

Before we get into the bibliographies though, it will be worthwhile to review the subject of libraries in general—how books are classified, how the card catalog is set up, and so on. A quick refamiliarization with the library now can save us much valuable time once we are there. To this end, one can hardly do better than to read the following excellent summary which was prepared by the United States Air Force Training Command for one of the courses given at the Air University:

Use of the Library

The plot of a Shakespearian play, a biographical sketch of Captain Cook or some other historical figure, the names of the ten largest cities in the United States, the date that California became a state—no matter what bit of general information you want, the first place you turn to is the public library. All of us have come to think of the library as the best, and often the only, source of needed knowledge. We know that its books, magazines, newspapers, and pamphlets are an inexhaustible reservoir of information and entertainment.

Yet even those of us who are at home in libraries often overlook services they provide other than those pertaining to reading. Large libraries have film and record collections; they offer the services of trained librarians who will assist you in special research and guide you to the library materials you need.

In fact, a person anxious to develop himself could hardly do better than to frequent his local library. By tapping its reservoir of information relating to his particular occupation, he can improve his job performance. In addition, he can use the library to become a more well-rounded person. By studying hobbies and creative arts, he can make his leisure hours more interesting and incidentally prepare himself for that seemingly distant day when he retires. The story of the retired person who becomes miserable because of inactivity has been told many times. Libraries can point the way to an adjusted retirement by giving us new interests outside our eight–five job.

To be sure, not all libraries overflow with materials. The size of the library depends (like practically everything else) on its financial support. In some cities, public-spirited citizens have endowed the public library. In others, the city government appropriates tax money. And of course, state colleges have libraries supported by state funds. Moreover, the extent of financial support goes back to the use which the people make of their library and to their desire for a good library. Community need is in turn related to the number of schools which need to supplement their own libraries with more extensive collections.

Public demand and funds likewise govern the hours of operation of most libraries. In most cities the library will be open from 9 in the morning to 9 at night. The library is usually centrally located for convenience for its users.

Having looked at libraries in a general sort of way, let's turn now to the specific practices followed by most of them. In other words, let's find out how to use the library to best advantage.

LIBRARY ARRANGEMENT

American libraries may differ in size, quality, the details of their arrangement, and their purpose, but certain elements are common to most systems, for example, reading rooms and book stacks. The reading room and circulation desk are usually located near the entrance to the building. At the circulation desk books are charged to and returned by the patrons Well-lighted and ventilated, the reading room contains tables and chairs so arranged that users can lay their work out in front of them.

The control of library materials is becoming fairly well standardized. One library will have about the same collections as any other library of the same size and type. Practically all libraries require that certain materials be used only in the library Periodicals, encyclopedias, reference books, documents, and valuable and rare items usually are so restricted.

A further control is occasionally applied to circulating books. Some libraries (to eliminate pilfering) store these volumes in closed-shelf stacks. Readers cannot go to these stacks but must ask the librarian to get the books for them. On the other hand, readers are welcome in open-shelf stacks, in which they may browse and select the books they want.

In any case, libraries have to follow a system in lending books. They first of all require that each borrower have a library card. If you are not a resident or a stranger in town, you may have to have a local property holder vouch for you. But if you are a resident, are listed in the city directory, or are otherwise identifiable, the library will issue a card. You will have to show this card every time you borrow a book. On college campuses, a similar system is followed, except that a new card is usually issued at the beginning of each semester. (At most colleges, use of the library is free to all regularly enrolled students.)

A charging system encouraged the prompt return of materials borrowed from the library. Failure to return books on or before the due date brings a fine of from 2 to 5 cents for each day they are overdue. Circulating books can usually be kept for a period of 2 weeks and are renewable for at least one additional period. However, if the books are in great demand, they are placed on the *reserve* shelf and issued either for use in the library or for overnight.

An *order department* is another necessary part of the library system. Trained personnel select new books and materials to be added.

When these new books come in they are turned over to the *cataloging department* to be stamped with the name of the library inside the back cover of the book. This department places a card pocket in it. When the book is ready for the shelves, it is numbered with the appropriate number and cataloged in the files. This catalog system will be discussed more fully in the next section.

CLASSIFICATION

To make books easy to find, libraries classify them into subject groups. Another reason for grouping books is that most readers prefer to have the books on the same subject located together so that they can examine the books themselves rather than search a list or file catalog. To satisfy these requirements, libraries group books according to the Dewey Decimal Classification system.

In decimal classification each class may be divided into ten divisions, each division into ten subdivisions, each subdivision into ten further ones. The ten main classes of the system are:

000 General Works
100 Philosophy
200 Religion
300 Social Sciences
400 Philology
500 Pure Science
600 Useful Arts
700 Fine Arts
800 Literature
900 History (including Biography, Description, and Travel)

Certain numbers divide material by form. The average person who wishes to become adept in the use of the library should start by memorizing the above ten classes. He should learn the divisions according to form, illustrated below.

01 Philosophy Theory
History falls in class 900—Philosophy of history 901
Science falls in class 500—Philosophy of science 501
Literature is in class 800—Philosophy of literature 801
Religion is in class 200—Philosophy of religion 201

02 Compendiums, handbooks, outlines
History falls in class 900—Outline of history 902
Religion falls in class 200—Outline of religion 202

03 Dictionaries, cyclopedias
Literature is in class 800—A dictionary of literature 803

04 Essays, addresses, lectures
Thus 404 essays on language
05 Periodicals
905 would be periodicals on history
06 Collective bodies, organizations, associations, societies —506 scientific society proceedings.
07 Study and teaching—A study of social science, 307; the teaching of literature, 807
08 Collections or extracts—A collection of literature, 808
09 History and general local treatment—A history of literature, 809

In classifying a book the librarian examines the book carefully to find out its subject, the author's purpose, and the class of readers, who will find it most useful. To do this, he reads the title page, preface, introduction, table of contents, and extracts from the book to determine its general class. Having found the class to which the book belongs, the librarian then refers to a table giving the subdivision numbers for that broad class. The science subdivisions are given below as an example.

500 Pure Science
510 Mathematics
520 Astronomy
530 Physics
540 Chemistry
550 Geology
560 Paleontology
570 Biology-Anthropology
580 Botany
590 Zoology

Now let's see how the decimal system is further applied. The class number is 900, and the table says that 900 is divided according to place and time. To classify the book, the librarian would have to know what country or section of a country the book is about, and if it covers the entire history of that country or only a specific period. The following examples may help you to understand the breakdown.

909 Coverage from the creation to the present time for the entire world (General)

940 History of Europe
England is always 2.—Therefore a history of England carries the number "942."
Germany is always 3.—Therefore a history of Germany carries the number "943."
France is always 4.—Therefore a history of France has the number "944."

A book with the number "973" covers only the history of the United States. How do we know? The figure "9" indicates that it is history, "7" that it is limited geographically to North America, and "3" that it is confined to the United States.

In the preceding paragraph we saw that books on history are classified according to place and time. Since we know how place is indicated, let's find out about the method of indicating time. Suppose, for example, we were classifying *History of the American Colonies* by M.W. Jernigan, which covers the period from 1492 to 1750. According to the divisions made by the Dewey System, the period of discovery and exploration is indexed as 973.1, and the colonial period as 973.2. However, because the book emphasizes the colonial period, the earlier period being treated only for background purposes, the more applicable number would be 973.2, the one representing the colonial history.

All subdivision numbers are indicated by decimals, like the .2 above. Suppose the librarian had to classify a book about radio stations. Even the librarian cannot carry all the numbers in his head; so he refers to the table for classification. He recognizes that engineering falls in the general class of *Useful Arts*, 600. Following down through the list, he finds that the figure 620 represents all general books on engineering. Still tracing the numbers, he finds something like this:

621.3 Electrical engineering
.38 Electric communication: telegrafy, telefony, wireless
.384 Wireless electric communications: telegrafy, telefony, radio

.3841 General questions, radio principles
.38416 Radio stations
.384164 Broadcasting stations
.38419 Applications
.384193 Broadcasting

He therefore numbered the book 621.38416 and placed it on the shelves.

The classification numbers may serve many purposes in the library. They are used to:

a. Arrange the books on the shelves logically.

b. Provide a brief and accurate call number for each book.

c. Locate a particular book on the shelf.

d. Provide a symbol for charging books to the user.

e. Simplify the work of the librarian in returning books to shelves.

f. Identify books during inventory.

THE CARD CATALOG

The card catalog is useful to anyone looking for books on a particular subject. By searching the catalog for source material, he can find whether there is material on the subject, and where it is located on the shelves. Although the librarian is always ready to help you, you can save his time and yours if you learn how to find your own material. You should therefore understand the card catalog before doing research.

This card catalog is usually located in the main reading room so as to be accessible to the people who will need to refer to it frequently. The cards within the drawers are arranged simply, most of them being alphabetized in a single sequence. The principal exceptions are:

a. Historical subjects are arranged in chronological sequence.

b. Abbreviations are filed as if they were spelled out.

c. Articles like "the" and "a" in a title are disregarded.

d. Names beginning with "Mc" are filed as though they began with "Mac."

e. The alphabet is followed word by word in filing rather than letter by letter.

There are at least three possible places in the card catalog where you may find the book that you are looking for. It may be found under the *last name of the author,* under the *title* of the book, or under the *subject* of the book. The main entry, however, is the author card, which contains further information.

The normal size of the cards found in the catalog is 3×5 inches. The card has the following information given in specified locations. Indentions and spacing make its use clear to the user.

a. Call Nr. This number is placed on the third line and second space from the left edge of the card. An identifying letter (the author's last initial) follows as part of the classification number.

b. Author's Name. The author's full name and date of birth is given on the 4th line and 1st indention (8th space from the left edge of the card). If the date of birth is followed by a dash, the author is still living.

c. Title. This is the line below the author's name and is indented (12th space from the left edge of the card). The title is reproduced from the title page exactly as stated.

d. Imprint. This is the place of publication, publisher, and date, exactly as they appear at the bottom of the title page. This is placed on the card 5 spaces after the period following the title if there is room; if not, at the first indention.

e. Collation. Gives the number of pages in the preface and the text with the height and size of the book, and information about illustrations.

f. Notes. Notes are added to explain the title or correct any misapprehension that might exist about it, and also to supply essential information about the author and bibliographical details not given in the title, imprint, or collation.

g. Contents. Publications that are not described sufficiently within the title that contain several works by the same author, or works by several authors, or works on several subjects, or a single work on a number of distinct subjects are shown in the contents.

In addition to author, title, and subject cards, the average card catalog has "cross-reference" cards. There are two kinds of cross-references.

a. The reader may be familiar with an author's pseudonym and not know his real name under which the book is entered in the card catalog. For example:

Twain, Mark
see
Clemens, Samuel Langhorne

b. The reader may find some material under the heading that was listed, but additional information on the same subject or related subjects may be referred to in the card shown. See the following example:

School libraries, see also
Children's Literature
Libraries, Children's
Libraries and Schools

PERIODICALS AND INDEXES

The card catalog frequently lists periodicals in the library, but seldom does it index the contents of these periodicals. To take care of this condition, cumulative indexes are issued in periodical and book form. The most useful periodical index is the *Readers' Guide,* published semimonthly and bound into monthly, semiannual, annual, and biennial volumes. This guide is an index to more than 100 America and Canadian periodicals that are found most frequently in American libraries and homes. All articles are alphabetically indexed under subject and author and in some cases under the title. You can locate a current article by looking under the letter of the alphabet corresponding with the author's initial. It is also possible to find articles on a subject, like "Tennessee Valley Authority," by looking under the letter "T."

To use the references from the index you must understand the standard form of reference. For example (Sci Am 149:843–5 Ag '33) means *Scientific American,* volume 149, pages 843 through 845 in the August 1933 issue.

Another index of equal importance is the *International Index.* This is a specialized periodical index of over 250 American and foreign magazines largely in the fields of science, language, literature, and history. It uses the same arrangement as the *Readers' Guide.* If a person understands the form of reference in one index, he can use the other.

In addition to these indexes, specialized indexes of periodicals are prepared for some fields, such as:

Education Index
Art Index
Industrial Arts Index (technology and business)
Public Affairs Information Service (Social Sciences)
Agriculture Index

Sometimes you may want to read critical opinions of a book or motion picture. *The Book Review Digest* summarizes the current books in a paragraph, followed by excerpts from other reviews that indicate whether the book was favorable or unfavorably received by the critics. *The Motion Picture Review Digest* analyzes films and comments as to their worth.

GENERAL REFERENCE BOOKS

A reference book covers a broad sweep of information. Just as its name implies, you refer to this type of book for specific information. Among the most commonly used reference books are dictionaries, encyclopedias, yearbooks, atlases, biographical dictionaries, and miscellaneous handbooks.

The two dictionaries in most common use are the *Merriam-Webster New International* and *Funk and Wagnalls New Standard.* These two dictionaries differ somewhat. One difference is that the Webster dictionary gives the oldest meaning of the word first whereas the Funk and Wagnall dictionary gives the most common meaning for the word first. The Oxford English Dictionary is valuable for its history of words and the approximately two million quotations taken from the literature of the English people used for illustrative purposes.

Especially good reference material is available in the encyclopedias found in most libraries. One of the best of these is the twenty-four volume *Encyclopedia Britannica.* If a person wants information on any of 460,000 subjects covered in the Britannica he should refer to the index in volume 24. The Britannica is kept up to date with an annual yearbook. Major revisions occur about every 10 years. The *Encyclopedia Americana* is a thirty-volume set that uses cross-references instead of the alphabetical index to locate topics for which there are no separate articles. Other encyclopedias that are especially good for school libraries are *Compton's Encyclopedia* and the *World Book.* In *Compton's* there is an index in the back of each volume, while the *World Book* uses the cross-reference scheme in its set.

The three most frequently used yearbooks are the *World Almanac,* the *Statesman's Yearbook,* and the *American Yearbook.* The *World Almanac* has a summary of facts and figures covering all phases of human activity during the preceding year. The *Statesman's Yearbook* discusses the governments of the world under three different areas: the British Empire, the United States and its possessions, and the rest of the world arranged in alphabetical sequence by country. The *American Yearbook* discusses and records the progress during the preceding year in the sciences, social sciences, arts, and humanities.

You often need to refer to a good atlas and gazetteer to locate cities, countries, rivers, etc. For the school library

Goode's School Atlas is probably one of the best. Larger libraries will probably have the larger and more complete *World Atlas.*

Or, if you want a thumbnail sketch of an important living American, you would probably refer to *Who's Who in America.* For information about famous Americans of the past, refer to the *Dictionary of American Biography.*

Here we have mentioned only a few of the hundreds of reference books found in most libraries. Reference books are usually kept separate from circulating books and are identified in the card catalog by an "R" preceding the call number. In addition, large libraries will often have a copy of Dr. Louis Shores' book, *Basic Reference Books.* Primarily a guide for setting up a reference department, this book nevertheless is helpful to the library user looking for particular types of reference books.

Of course, we don't want to rely exclusively on public libraries for our reading. Most of us like to build a practical library for our own use. This should include references that fit the special needs of the individual. In addition to these references everyone needs a good desk dictionary. A book of synonyms and antonyms is another useful book. If the work of the person requires that he conduct a certain amount of business by correspondence he should buy a handbook of English usage. A world atlas is convenient for locating places for business or professional reasons and should be part of every person's library.

Now we are ready for those bibliographies:

The first bibliography is a *general* guide to sources for genealogical research. Most of these books direct you to primary genealogical data; that is, to the original records and files of the United States, at local town, city and nationwide levels. The *Guide to Genealogical Records in the National Archives,* to cite one instance, tells the researchers what kinds of United States records of military service are available, what types of genealogical data they include, and where in the Archives they are located. Other sources in this list serve as indexes or catalogs to previously published genealogies. This selective bibliography is basic to any beginning researcher.

After this initial introduction to available genealogical records, you are probably anxious to delve into the printed history of your particular family. We compiled our second bibliography with this end in mind. These books on heraldry and surname histories allow the researcher to better understand his family origins. Beyond your own specific purpose of gaining more knowledge about your family and its traditions, the sources included in this list help you to place your family within an historical context. The information they provide is invaluable in the process of tracing your ancestry.

These first two bibliographies may perhaps seem obvious sources to even the beginning genealogist; but the thorough researcher never overlooks even the obvious. Both of these bibliographies serve as a sound and necessary background to further your genealogical study. The stronger and more thorough your initial research is, the easier and more competent your extended research will be.

The third bibliography provided in this section is a great aid in making available to you material that contains a vast amount of genealogical data. This bibliography presents names of periodical indexes. These indexes were compiled with the genealogist in mind, and so help to arrange data that might otherwise be forgotten. With the use of such an index you can more easily determine which particular issues of these journals may be of value to you on your hunt.

The fourth and final bibliography contains a variety of books supplying genealogical data, or directing you to the original sources of that data. This compilation also serves to remind the novice researcher of the wide spectrum of sources from which genealogical information can be derived. Whether from church records, county records, or United States census records, most often the information is there to be examined, but it is up to the inventive genealogist to make use of it.

And, hopefully, these four bibliographies will help you to overcome many of the obstacles which typically plague beginners. Initially, if the four different types of sources are used one step at a time, your search in the library will not be a chaotic and overwhelming problem, but rather a pleasurable and profitable learning process. While these four compilations are intended to increase your awareness of the magnitude of possible sources of data, they are also limited in number in order to give the vast realm of data workable boundaries. All four bibliographies have been selected on the basis of historical accuracy, reliability, and validity. You can use just one category at a time, but more likely, after you are familiar with them, you'll find it useful to work all four categories at once in a process of cross-referencing a theory or fact, or in discovering new pieces of information. These bibliographies provide a starting point for your genealogical work in the library. With a careful scrutiny of some or all of these works and an inquisitive spirit, you are off to an excellent start in making the library meet its full potential for you.

Where to begin your search? Without a guide or sense of direction, the genealogical search appears to be an insurmountable problem. For this reason we have included the following bibliographical list; it serves as an aid to the beginning genealogist in his understanding of the reasons and methods for planned, competent research. The sources mentioned are significant instruments in helping you begin your project with an understanding of the possible problems that may arise and with answers to those problems. This selected bibliography is in essence an index and catalog to genealogical records located in the Library of Congress and National Archives, as well as in many public libraries. It can help you to familiarize yourself with what types of genealogical sources are available, where they can be found, and how they can best be utilized. Hopefully, it will serve to expand your awareness of the magnitude of sources that are, in fact, available to the industrious and inquiring genealogist, yet at the same time give you that initial step essential to direct your research.

American Genealogical Index. New series. Vol. 1—. Middletown, Conn.: Godfrey Memorial Library, 1952—.

Carroll, Mrs. Riernan J. "Sources for Genealogical Research in State Department Records." *National Genealogical Society Quarterly* 52 (December 1964).

Colket, Meredith B., Jr., and Bridgers, F.E. *Guide to Genealogical Records in the National Archives.* Washington, D.C.: Superintendent of Documents, 1964.

Glenn, Thomas A. *A List of Some American Genealogies Which Have Been Printed in Book Form.* Philadelphia, 1897. Reprint. Baltimore: Genealogical Publishing Co., 1969.

Kaminkow, Marion. *Genealogies in the Library of Congress: A Bibliography.* 2 vols. Baltimore: Magna Carta, 1972.

Library of Congress. *American and English Genealogies in the Library of Congress.* 2nd ed., 1919. Reprint. Baltimore: Genealogical Publishing Co. 1967. (Information in this volume is kept current on microcards published by Godfray Memorial Library, Middletown, Connecticut.)

Long Island Historical Society. *Catalog of the American Genealogies in the Library.* Prepared under the direction of the librarian, Emma Toedteberg. Brooklyn, New York: 1935. Reprint. Baltimore: Genealogical Publishing Co., 1969.

Major Genealogical Record Sources in the United States. A Guide to Major Sources and Their Availability. Genealogical Society of the Church of Jesus Christ of Latter Day Saints, circ. research paper, series B, no. 1. Salt Lake City: The Society, 1967.

Munsell's, Joel, Sons. *The American Genealogist, Being a Catalogue of Family Histories. A Bibliography of American Genealogy, or a List of the Title Pages of Books or Pamphlets on Family History, Published in America From 1771 to Date (1900).* 5th ed. 1900. Reprint. Detroit: Gale Research, 1967. Baltimore: Genealogical Publishing Co., 1967.

Munsell's, Joel, Sons. *Index to American Genealogies; and to Genealogical Material Contained in All Works . . . With (Suppl.) 1900-1908 to the Index to Genealogies Alphabetically Arranged.* 5th ed rev., improved, and enlarged, 1900. Supplement, 1900-1908. Reprint. Detroit: Gale Research, 1967. Baltimore: Genealogical Publishing Co., 1967.

Newberry Library, Chicago. *The Genealogical Index.* 4 vols. Boston: G.K. Hall, 1960.

Perkins, Marvin E. "Genealogical Problems in the Light of Contemporary Psychology." *National Genealogical Society Quarterly* 47 (June 1959).

Rider, Fremont, ed. *American Genealogical Index.* 48 vols. Middletown, Connecticut: 1942-1952.

Rubincam, Milton. *Genealogy: A Selected Bibliography*. Prepared for the Institute of Genealogy, Samford University, Alabama. Birmingham: Banner Press, 1967.

Smith, Elsdon C. *Personal Names: A Bibliography*. 1952. Reprint. Detroit: Gale Research, 1967.

Chapter 10 of this book discusses in detail the field of heraldry. The works listed below are intended to help the interested genealogist further extend his study of the subject. The majority of listed works are easy to read and use as heraldic guides. Many of the books include illustrations of the coats of arms as well as indexes arranged by surname. This authoritative listing serves not only to help you find your family's coat of arms, but also to expound on the development of evolution of heraldry as detailed in Chapter 10.

Adam, Frank. *The Clans, Septs, and Regiments of the Scottish Highlands*. Revised by Sir Thomas Innes of Learney. 4th ed. Edinburgh: W & A Johnston, 1952.

Anglo-Jewish Notabilites: Their Arms and Testamentary Dispositions. London: Jewish Historical Society of England, 1949.

Appleton, William S. *The Gore Roll of Arms and Positive Pedigrees and Authorized Arms*. Baltimore: Heraldic Book Co., 1964.

Bolton, Charles Knowles. *Bolton's American Armory*. Baltimore: Genealogical Publishing Co., 1969.

Burke, Sir Bernard. *Burke's Genealogical and Heraldic History of the Landed Gentry of Ireland*. Edited by L.G. Pine. 4th ed. London: Burke's Peerage, 1968.

Burke, Sir Bernard. *The General Armory of England, Scotland, Ireland, and Wales*. London: 1884. Reprint. Baltimore: Genealogical Publishing Co., 1969.

Child, Heather. *Heraldic Design: A Handbook for Students*. London: G. Bell and Sons, 1965.

Committee on Heraldry. *Roll of Arms*. Boston: New England Historic Genealogical Society, 1936.

Crozier, William Armstrong, ed. *Crozier's General Armory, a Register of American Families Entitled to Coat Armor*. Baltimore: Genealogical Publishing Co., 1966.

Fairbairn, James. *Book of Crests of the Families of Great Britain and Ireland*. 4th ed. Baltimore: Heraldic Book Co., 1968.

Ferguson, Joan P.S. *Scottish Family Histories Held in Scottish Libraries.* Edinburgh: Scottish Central Library, 1960.

Filby, P. William, comp. *American and British Genealogy and Heraldry, a Selected List of Books.* Chicago: American Library Assoc., 1970.

Fox-Davies, Arthur Charles, ed. *Armorial Families: a Dictionary of Gentlemen of Coat-Armour.* 2 vols. Rutland, Vermont: Charles E. Tuttle Co., 1970.

Gatfield, George. *Guide to Printed Books and Manuscripts Relating to English and Foreign Heraldry and Genealogy.* Detroit: Gale Research, 1966.

Gayre of Gayre and Nigg, Robert and Gayre and Gayre and Nigg, Reinold. *Roll of Scottish Arms.* London: The Amorial, 1964.

Innes, Sir Thomas. *The Tartans of the Clans and Families of Scotland.* 6th ed. Edinburgh: Johnston, 1958.

Matthews, John. *Complete American Armory and Blue Book.* New York: Heraldic Publishing Co., 1965.

Moule, Thomas. *Bibliotheca Heraldica Magnae Britanniae: An Analytical Catalogue of Books on Genealogy, Heraldry, Nobility, Knighthood and Ceremonies from 1469-1821, and a Supplement Enumerating the Principal Foreign Genealogical Works.* New York: Barnes and Noble, 1966.

Papworth, John W. *An Alphabetical Dictionary of Coats and Arms Belonging to Families of Great Britain and Ireland; Forming an Extensive Ordinary of British Armorials.* 2 vols. Baltimore: Genealogical Publishing Co., 1965.

Rietstap, Jean Baptiste. *Armorial General: Precede d'un Dictionaire des Termes du Blason.* 2 vols. 2nd ed. New York: Barnes and Noble, 1965.

Stephenson, Jean. *Heraldry For the American Genealogist.* Special Publication No. 25. Washington, D.C.: National Genealogical Society, 1959.

Stuart, Margaret. *Scottish Family History: A Guide to Works of Reference on the History and Genealogy of Scottish Families.* Edinburgh: Oliver and Boyd, 1930.

Wagner, Sir Anthony R. *Aspilogia: A Catalogue of English Medieval Rolls of Arms.* London and New York: Oxford University Press, 1950.

Whitemore, W.H., ed. *The Heraldic Journal: Recording the Armorial Bearings and Genealogies of American Families.* 4 vols. 1865-68. Reprint (4 vols. in 1). Baltimore: Genealogical Publishing Co., 1972.

Vast numbers of genealogical periodicals which cover a wide spectrum of biographical data have been published throughout the years of American history. Unfortunately, because the task of sorting through these periodicals can be an overwhelming one, this extensive storehouse of historical and genealogical information is often neglected by the researcher; however, many genealogical societies and state institutions have indexed these periodicals, usually by surnames, article titles, and/or subjects. The following bibliographical list includes the names of some of the most reliable and most comprehensive indexes. These periodical indexes are a great timesaver for the researcher and help to make available material that otherwise would be too voluminous to sort through. With as little starting information as a family name or possibly even just a location and date, the use of one or more of these indexes can prove beneficial in finding the key that will unlock the door to your family's ancestry.

Adams, James N., comp. *General Index to the Journal of the Illinois State Historical Society, Volumes 1-25*. Springfield: The Society, 1949.

Barber, Gertrude A., comp. *Subject Index of the New York Genealogical and Biographical Record, Volumes 39-76 Inclusive.* New York: The Author, 1946.

Brigham, Clarence S. *History and Bibliography of American Newspapers, 1690-1820*. 2 vols. Worcester, Mass.: 1947.

Cappon, Lester J. *American Genealogical Periodicals: A Bibliography with a Chronological Finding-List*. New York: New York Public Library, 1962.

Columbia Library Club, comp. *The Missouri Historical Index: Volumes 1-25*. Columbia: The State Historical Society of Missouri, 1934.

Cruise, Boyd, comp. *Index to the Louisiana Historical Quarterly.* New Orleans: Plantation Bookshop, 1956.

Daughters of the American Revolution. *Genealogical Guide. Master Index of Genealogy in the DAR Magazine, vols. 1-84, 1892-1950*. Washington, D.C.: Daughters of the American Revolution, 1951.

Doll, Eugene E., ed. *The Pennsylvania Magazine of History and Biography: Index, Volumes 1-75*. Philadelphia: The Historical Society of Pennsylvania, 1954.

Fisher, Carlton E. *Topical Index, Vols. 1-50, 1912-1962.* National Genealogical Society, special pub. 29. Washington, D.C.: The Society, 1964.

Genealogical Periodical Annual Index, Vols. 1—, 1962—. Bladensburg, Md.: Ellen S. Rogers. Bowie, Md.: George E. Russell.

Gerould, Winifred. *American Newspapers, 1821-1936. A Union List of Files Available in the United States and Canada.* New York: 1937.

Gregory, James P., Jr., comp. *Missouri Historical Review: Cumulative Index to Volumes 26-45.* Columbia: The State Historical Society of Missouri, 1955.

Index to the Wisconsin Magazine of History, Volumes 26-35. Madison: The State Historical Society of Wisconsin, 1955.

Jacobus, Donald L. *Index to Genealogical Periodicals.* Vol. 1, 1858-1931; vol. 2, 1932-1946; vol. 3, 1947-1952. Reprint. Baltimore: Genealogical Publishing Co., 1963-65.

Krueger, Lillian, comp. *The Wisconsin Magazine of History: Index, Volumes 1-15.* Madison: The State Historical Society of Wisconsin, 1934.

Parsons, Margaret Wellington, ed. *Index (Abridged) to the New England Historical and Genealogical Register: Volumes 51 through 112.* Marlborough, Massachusetts: The Author, 1959.

Riker, Dorothy, comp. *Indiana Magazine of History: General Index, Volumes 1-25.* 1930. Reprint. New York: Kraus Reprint Corp., 1967.

Royne, Josephine E., and Chapman, Effie L., eds. *New England Historical and Genealogical Register: Index of Persons, Subjects, Places, Vols. 1-50.* 3 vols 1906-1911. Reprint. Baltimore: GPC, 1972.

Russell, George E. *Genealogical Periodicals Annual Index.* Vol. 5—, 1966—. Bowie, Md.: The Author, 1967—.

Spear, Dorothea N. *Bibliography of American Directories Through 1860.* Worcester, Massachusetts: American Antiquarian Society, 1961.

Supplement to Genealogical Guide: Master Index of Genealogy in the DAR Magazine, Vols. 85-89, 1950-1955. Washington, D.C.: Daughters of the American Revolution, 1956.

Swem, E.G., comp. *Virginia Historical Index.* Gloucester, Mass.: Peter Smith, 1965.

Waldenmaier, Inez. *Annual Index to Genealogical Periodicals and Family Histories.* Vols. for 1956-1962. Washington, D.C.

Youngs, Florence E. *Subject Index of the New York Genealogical & Biographical Record, Vols. 1-38.* New York. 1907.

Often it is easy to overlook sources which are of primary importance; the lay researcher is either not aware that these sources exist or he just does not know where they can be located. The bibliography listed below includes some of these valuable records which are, in fact, available at many local libraries. These sources include data about territorial divisions, land ownership, church denominations, and local histories. For instance, *The Territorial Papers as a Source for the Genealogist,* by Clarence E. Carter, Sr., provides a list of appointees to local and county offices as well as an indexed list of land claimants. Another interesting source which discloses much informative genealogical data is Kirkham's *A Survey of American Church Records.* This work gives a state-by-state breakdown of church records at the county, town, or city level. The following listing is intended to provide the researcher with genealogical sources that might have been neglected and, in addition, prompt the beginning genealogist to probe all possible avenues of research.

"Availability of Federal Mortality Census Schedules, 1850-1885." *National Genealogical Society Quarterly 52* (December 1964).

"Availability of Names Indexes to Federal Population Census Schedules, 1790-1890." *National Genealogical Society Quarterly* 51 (September 1963).

Bradford, Thomas C. *The Bibliographer's Manual of American History, Containing an Account of All States, Territories, Towns, and County Histories . . . With Verbatim Copies of the Titles, and Useful Bibliographical Notes.* Ed. and rev. by Stan V. Henkels. 1907-1910. Reprint (5 vols.) Detroit: Gale Research, 1968.

Carter, Clarence E., Sr. "The Territorial Papers as a Source for the Genealogist." *National Genealogical Society Quarterly* 37 (December 1949).

Child, Sargent B., and Holmes, D.P. *A Bibliography of Research Projects Reports. Checklist of Historical Records Survey Publications, Technical Series, Research and Records Bibliographies,* 7. Rev. ed. Washington, D.C.: 1943.

Crowther, George R., III. *Surname Index to Sixty-five Volumes of Colonial and Revolutionary Pedigrees.* National Genealogical Society special publ. 27. Washington, D.C.: The Society, 1964.

Franklin, W. Neil. "Availability of Federal Population Census

Schedules in the States." *National Genealogical Society Quarterly* 50 (March and June 1962).

Hale, Richard W. *Guide to Photocopied Historical Materials in the United States and Canada.* Ithaca: Cornell University Press for the American Historical Association, 1961.

Hamer, Philip M. *A Guide to Archives and Manuscripts in the United States.* New Haven: Yale University Press, 1961.

Kirkham, E. Kay. *A Survey of American Census Schedules; an Explanation and Description of our Federal Census Enumerations 1790 to 1950.* Salt Lake City: Deseret Book Co., 1959.

Library of Congress. Map Division. *A List of Geographical Atlases in the Library of Congress.* Vol. 1—, 1909—. Washington, D.C. Reprint (vols. 1-4). New York: Paladin Press, 1968.

Matthews, William, et al. *American Diaries . . . an Annotated Bibliography of American Diaries Written Prior to 1861.* Reprint. Boston: Canner, 1959.

Stephenson, Richard W. *Land Ownership Maps: A Checklist of Nineteenth Century United States County Maps in the Library of Congress.* Washington, D.C.: Superintendent of Documents, 1967.

A Survey of American Church Records. 2 vols. Salt Lake City: Deseret Book Company, 1959.

6

LOCAL RECORDS

Paul C. Larsen

One of the most important areas of your research will be in the official records generally located in town and county courthouses throughout the country. If used correctly, they will provide you with invaluable information in tracing your family tree. They can supply you with the name of a previously unknown ancestor, establish proof of your own descent, and also afford you a brief and unique lesson in American history.

Any one of three methods can be used to acquire these records. If you are undertaking your own research and can arrange a personal visit to the courthouse containing records pertinent to your family, you will be rewarded in several ways. There is nothing more gratifying to the genealogical researcher than to discover the vital statistics of a relative who lived more than a century ago. The search necessary to accomplish this task leads the investigator through folio-size, bound volumes called *libers,* which are legal and historical witnesses to how man has lived in the past. Early records, those dating before about 1800, are written by hand and sometimes employ archaic language. Your own inquiry into them will be a fascinating experience.

The second method of obtaining official records is by mail. If you do not live near the courthouse where they are kept, you can write the clerk of the court and ask him if he will conduct a search. This method is often thwarted by the fact that many town and county officials simply do not have the time or the manpower to follow through on your request.

However, should you be fortunate enough to find a clerk who can help you, it is important to be very clear in stating the questions you wish answered. Include the exact type of information you are requesting (such as birth, marriage, or death records) and any dates which might be helpful. It is always a good idea to offer payment for any fees the clerk may charge and to include a self-addressed, stamped envelope for his reply. Keep your letter of request as short and precise as possible. The following letter is one which brought its writer a successful reply:

> I am searching for the confirmed record of my great-grand-father's birth and marriage. His name was Joseph Walker and he is believed to have married in your town before 1840. His birth, also in your town, probably occurred about 1810 or 1815. Enclosed is an envelope for your reply and I will be happy to pay any fee you may charge for searching your records.

The final method of gathering information from official records is perhaps more for the spectator than for the participant. This is hiring a professional genealogist or title searcher who will perform the task for a fee (which is usually quite substantial).

By the time it becomes necessary for you to conduct your search, you will probably have already compiled information from other sources such as your own family and the local library. This information will have provided you with a basic knowledge of your pedigree, even though you may still lack a generation or two. It is now time to turn to the official records.

You will approach this body of information from one of two directions. Either you know that a certain ancestor had occasion to be entered into the records of a particular town or county during a specific year, or you suspect this might be the case because your family has been located in that town or county for a number of generations. Your search will begin in the office of the clerk of court, the recorder of deeds, or some similar official charged with the care and compilation of legal records. In some New England states such as Vermont, Connecticut, and Rhode Island, the local land records are filed in the individual towns of the state. While this is generally true of most states, others such as Pennsylvania, Maryland, Virginia, North and South Carolina, and Georgia, keep records in the State Archival Depository.

Once you have ascertained that you are in the right place, your next step will be to find the *surname index*. This index, although not present in all record offices, will serve as your roadmap through the miles of collected data. If the office does not contain a general index, there will probably be an index in the front of each bound volume, listing the names of the persons whose records are filed within. Each volume usually corresponds to a particular year, or part of a year. If you have a fairly good idea of the year in which an ancestor had official business, this index will provide you with a short-cut through the entire volume.

OFFICIAL COURT RECORDS

Now, to the records themselves! Court records can be divided into two categories: criminal and civil. Criminal records speak for themselves, and although they are usually of little value to the genealogist, they should be consulted if all other avenues of research prove unsuccessful. Civil records pertain to actions between private parties, as heard before probate, equity, and superior courts. They are categorized into files, dockets, registers of action, minutes, reporters' transcripts, orders of the court, and exhibits. Each should be examined. It is in the area of civil records that the greatest amount of genealogical information will be found. The three types of records which are of the most value to the genealogist are *land, vital,* and *probate.*

Local land records usually connote *deeds* in most people's minds. But deeds are only one part of these records and information is often found in mortgages, leases, liens, contracts, powers of attorney, releases, notices of action, judgments, and decrees. What kind of information can you hope to find in these records? Some records show the date when a person first entered a county and the name of the county and state from which he came. The deed for a piece of land is usually held in the name of the husband and his wife. The transfer of land, either by will or by sale, results in a record of the transaction. This record will include the man's name and the given name of his wife. This information is sometimes found only in the minutes of the court. When land is divided among heirs, the researchers can sometimes locate the names of all children, the places of their residence, and the names of the husbands of the married daughters. A single deed may be all you need to fill in an entire family group sheet.

Also, while examining deeds of your family, do not neglect to investigate how the grantor first came to own the land for which he holds the deed. It may be a simple case of his purchase, but then again, he may have inherited it by descent from the previous owner. If so, a genealogical fact will be made known to you. This raises an important point which should be considered when searching deeds. For the genealogist, the most helpful document is the *multiple-grantor deed.* This is a record of a deceased father's property being sold by his children. On such a record are the names of the sons, usually listed in order of birth, the names of the daughters and the names of their husbands, should they be married. Sometimes the deed will include the residence of each person and even their previous residences.

VITAL STATISTICS

Records which deal with the vital statistics of an individual are those which verify the place and date of someone's birth, marriage, and death. It is best to consult these documents when proof of a locality or a date for an ancestor is needed in completing your family tree. Work with these records in the past has indicated the need to adopt a uniform type of certificate which applies to all of them throughout the United States. This was done in recent years and today the records are registered in one central location. Duplicate copies or originals can be found in the town, county, or city where the birth, marriage, or death occurred.

While examining these records, remember that a marriage license is different than a marriage record. Licenses are usually issued by the county clerk, whereas marriage records are usually filed with the county recorder.

THE PROBATE RECORDS

The records which are of the greatest aid to the genealogist are the *probate records.* These are generally found in the index called "Index to Administrations and Estates." The most important category of these records is the last will and testament. Wills are of great genealogical value because they are almost always indisputable documents concerning the relationship of individuals. In legal language, the "will" is a document which disposes of real estate and the "testament" is a document which disposes of personal property. It is in this area of family records that you should be most careful in your examination, for not only do wills convey the greatest amount of familial information, but errors of omission by clerks copying the records are fairly common. Also, other papers pertaining to the same estate may be included in the will such as inventories, renunciations of a widow, guardianships of minors, accounts, and distributions. These papers may also contain genealogical facts.

There are two types of wills: a written will, signed and witnessed; and the *nuncupative will,* an oral statement declared by the testator (the person making the will) in presence of witnesses. Although nuncupative wills are rare in the twentieth century, they were common during the settling of this country, when writing material was not always available and many people did not know how to write.

There are a number of legal questions which arise involving wills. Because probate laws are different in each state, you would be wise to look into the laws of your state. This not only may save time, but it will also broaden your knowledge of civil records. In most states, however, there are some terms which are generally applied to probate cases. The disposition of an estate is usually determined by the will of the deceased. If the will is declared legal and binding, it it known as *testate*. If the deceased left no written will nor declarative statement, it is said that he died *intestate*. In this case, an administrator is appointed by the court to distribute the property of the deceased. The administrator is required by law to account for all property in the estate. In this accounting, the names of the heirs are listed, and if the heirs were descendants of the testator, a good amount of information can be found. Another source of material is the record of any litigation which might have occurred over an estate. Filed with other records and sometimes difficult to locate, these documents nevertheless might provide the names and perhaps the addresses of relatives. For instance, a paper seemingly as insignificant as the renunciation of a widow to serve as administratix, may be the only evidence of the first name of the widow.

After the death of the testator, an executor of the testate will is appointed. The executor is a person named in the will and appointed by the court to carry out the provisions of the will. He probates (proves) the will by bringing it before the court with the witnesses who testify that they were present when the will was signed. If the will was nuncupative, the witnesses testify that they were present when the oral statement was made. If the court judges the matter to be legal and proper, it will issue testamentary letters authorizing the executor to proceed with the wishes of the deceased. These should be examined for any genealogical material they might contain.

Wills are not the only documents which are included in probate records. There are also petitions for probate of will, petitions for letters of administration, notices to creditors, affidavits, letters testamentary granted by the court to the executor, letters of administration (same as letters testamentary, except they are granted to an administrator of an intestate will), bonds of executor or administrator, and inventories and appraisements. None of these records should be overlooked in your research.

The courts which have jurisdiction over probate matters are different from state to state. Alabama and Arkansas keep their records in probate courts, but New York and New Jersey records are found in the surrogate's court. Other states appoint the superior court or the circuit courts as custodian. A number of cities deposit their records with the register of wills.

The language of wills, particularly very old wills, is sometimes misleading. There is an excellent treatment of this subject of language usage changes in Chapter 3, and it is strongly recommended that you familiarize yourself with that before trying to tackle an old document.

INFORMATION ON WILLS

Throughout history wills have been the most precise statement of family relationships. Usually a man will name his wife, his children (in order of birth), his grandchildren, and sometimes his collateral relatives. Wills are generally thought to be a source of proof of descent, rather than ascent, but occasionally the parentage of the testator is given in the will. Unmarried and childless men often name their brothers and sisters, uncles, aunts, and cousins. Of course not all wills are so specific, and you may find one which offers nothing more than "all my property is to be released to my wife and son." Wills as succinct as this were not uncommon during the early days of this country.

After you have examined the land, vital, and probate records which you believe might contain information about your family, you still have several other valuable sources to investigate. Because this is a nation in which almost every personal transaction goes on paper, it is reasonable to assume that there is somewhere a record of an ancestor you are searching. Buried in the files of many courts throughout the country are depositions, records of lawsuits, and other court actions which contain clues to the identity of people who have lived in the past. Some of these files are the result of a criminal case, and while the genealogical information contained in them may be miniscule, they should all be examined. Other files contain the transcripts from lawsuits over the distribution of an estate or the contest of a will. These will include information almost as valuable as the will itself.

THE SHRIEVE CASE By way of a practical illustration as to the location and the use of official records, a friend of ours recently recounted his own search in the office of the clerk of court in Alexandria, Virginia. David Shrieve is a resident of this city, one of the oldest in the country, surveyed by George Washington in July 1749. Dave told us that compilation of the records began in 1783. Today Alexandria is an independent city, but her history has seen several changes which have affected genealogical research. Like many towns, counties, cities, and even states, Alexandria's borders have been rearranged several times in the past two centuries. Originally annexed as a section of Washington, D.C., her records were kept as a part of that jurisdiction. In the middle of the nineteenth century, the town (her official designation at that time) became a part of Arlington County, Virginia. These changes tend to confuse the researcher. If an ancestor was born in 1806 in Washington, D.C., it is possible that his records might have been filed in the Alexandria office. If the modern researcher is not aware of the jurisdictional changes, he might believe that no record exists after locating nothing in the Washington records. This is a very important point to keep in mind when you are conducting your own research. Be sure to study the history of the location you are investigating for possible boundary changes.

After speaking with the clerk for several minutes, Dave was able to learn that this office neither conducts genealogical research nor fills requests by mail. The reason for this is a lack of funds and limited staff. The clerk did offer, however, to refer Dave to several local genealogists or title searchers. But Dave assured him that he wanted to undertake his own research and asked him for access to the records. Although no index is kept by the office, there is in front of each volume an index to the records bound inside. Dave related that these indexes were quite helpful in his research on the Shrieve family.

He was able to locate his great-grandfather, Thomas A. Shrieve, in the records. Thomas' birth was on 15 May 1811, and this date is recorded in the Alexandria courthouse and also in the State Archival Depository in Richmond, the capital of Virginia. Because the birth certificate indicated Jeremiah and Martha Shrieve as the parents, Dave was able to locate one more generation of his family. After searches through several other records books, Dave found the will of Jeremiah Shrieve. Dated in 1828, it leaves a house and approximately two acres of land to Martha Shrieve, Thomas A. Shrieve, and Joseph Shrieve. This information somewhat startled our friend, for until then he was unaware he had a great-great-uncle. With the location of two records books, Dave was able to find the names and addresses of five members of his family.

From here his next step was to check the marriage records in the years between 1828 (at which time Thomas was seventeen) and 1838. His reasoning for this was that if Thomas got married, he probably did so in that decade. He found that in 1832 there was a listing for the marriage of Thomas Shrieve and Sarah Carter. But he also found a listing for a Thomas Shrieve and a Mary Watson, married in 1836. As neither contained the initial "A," Dave was unable to determine proof of his great-grandfather's marriage. Further research was needed.

Because Dave did not know the death date of Thomas and thus realized his will would be difficult to locate, he decided to consult the local land records. Dave knew that Thomas had inherited a part of his father's property in 1828 and that he would be considered a co-owner with his mother and brother. Searching the index of land records from that date to 1832, the time of the first marriage he had located, Dave came across no deed to the property. Although discouraged, he remembered our advice to consult as many records as possible. It then occurred to him that because Mrs. Shrieve was an owner, she would dispose of this estate in her will. A search in the death records of the office was successful—Mrs. Martha Shrieve died on 23 October 1833. Her will was probated during the first month of 1834. It stipulated that one-half of the property be assigned to Thomas and Sarah Shrieve and one-half to Joseph and Susan Shrieve. Dave now had proof of his great-grandfather's marriage and he also had discovered his great-great-aunt.

This is just one example illustrating the worth of official records. In one morning our friend had collected enough evidence to prove the descent of two generations of his family. His research also made him aware of the passage of time in two ways: each of the records Dave consulted was written in hand and each contained archaic spellings and language. He also discovered that much of the legal terminology citied in the deeds, wills, and other records had changed very little over the centuries.

Dave's research and his very important findings point out the importance of official records. Although Dave admitted that he had never spent much time researching his family tree, he several times commented on how easy he found his search in the courthouse. Certainly his success stimulated his interest, but he said he felt that the mere adventure of his search would have been enough to prompt him to additional research.

Dave's story serves as an example of how the uninitiated can become fascinated by their own part in the developing family tree. The local records which he discovered will now be made available to his children, and probably to their children. The story also serves to illustrate the fact that many records lie on shelves of courthouses throughout the country, ready for a researcher to tap their valuable information.

The following is a glossary of legal terms often encountered in record research. We add them here to help you with your research at the courthouse.

administration: the management and settling of an estate.

administrator: a person appointed by a court to settle the estate of a deceased person who has died without leaving a valid will.

affidavit: a signed written statement sworn before a notary or other court officer.

assignee: one to whom some right, privilege, or property is signed over by the court.

assignor: one who signs over the title or interest in something (e.g., a part or whole of an estate) to another individual or party.

bequest: commonly used to denote a gift of real estate by will; also a legacy.

bounty land: land given by the government to induce men to enter military service; it usually consisted of a specific number of acres of previously unallocated public land.

bounty land warrant: a gift of bounty land due a person, his heirs, or assigns and entitled by military service.

canon law: a law or statute of the church.

collateral ancestor: an ancestor not in direct line of ascent, but of the same ancestral stock (e.g. the brother or sister of a direct ancestor).

consanguinity: relation by blood; descended from a common ancestor.

decedent: a deceased person.

deed: a formal written instrument, signed, sealed and delivered according to law and conveying title to real estate.

denizen: a person who has been admitted to residence in a foreign country.

deposition: the testimony of a witness in writing and duly authenticated, given in the course of a legal proceeding.

direct heir: one who is an individual's direct line of ascent or descent.

descendant: one who is descended, however remotely, from another.

devise: to grant real property by will.

devisee: one to whom real property is given by will.

dower: the legal right of a wife to use or own some portion of her husband's real estate, should she survive him.

escheat: reverting of property to the state upon the death of an owner without heirs.

estate: the property of a deceased person: a right, title, or interest in that property.

executor: the person named in a will and appointed by a court to carry out the provisions of the will.

executrix: feminine form of executor.

fee simple: an estate of inheritance in land, absolute and without limitation to any particular class of heirs.

fee tail: an estate of inheritance in land, limited to a particular class of heirs.

freeholder: a person who held land in fee simple. He had the right to vote and hold public office.

grant: a term used in deeds for transferring title to real property.

grantee: one to whom a grant is made.

grantor: one who makes a grant (e.g. transfers title to real property).

guardian: a person appointed by a court to care for the property and rights of a minor or someone otherwise incapable of administering his own affairs.

heir: a person who by descent or right of relationship inherits an estate upon the death of his ancestor.

holographic will: a will entirely in the handwriting of the testator.

imprimis: "first of all."

indenture: any deed, written contract, or sealed agreement; a contract by which a person, as an apprentice, is bound over for service; the formal agreement between a group of bondholders and the debtor as to the terms of the debt.

infant: a person not of legal age; a minor.

intestate: a person who has died without having left a valid will or otherwise disposed of his real and personal property.

inventory: a list of goods or valuables in the estate of a deceased person, filed in probate court by an executor or administor.

kindred: persons related by blood.

legacy: a gift by will.

lineal descendant: a person in the direct line of descent.

nuncupative will: an oral or unwritten will, declared by the testator in his last sickness and in the presence of witnesses, and later reduced to writing by someone other than the testator.

posthumous: born after the father's death.

personal property: all property other than real property.

primogeniture: condition of being the first-born child of the same parents: in law, the right of inheritance by the eldest son.

probate: the process of proving a will.

relicit: a widow; sometimes (rarely) used to mean a widower.

sibling: a brother or sister; all children of the same parents.

spouse: a husband or wife.

trustee: a person to whom another's property or the management of another's property is given in trust.

testate: having made or left a valid will.

testator: a man who died leaving a valid will.

testatrix: feminine form of testator.

testament: the disposition of one's personal property by will.

will: the legal document containing the statement of a person's wishes regarding the disposal of his property after his death.

7

STATE RECORDS

AGRI Staff

Like local records, the records of the various states are veritable treasure troves of information, and, at some point or another in his search, nearly every genealogist finds himself pursuing this line of inquiry. For your convenience, the staff of the American Genealogical Research Institute has compiled an alphabetical state-by-state listing of the appropriate offices to contact for genealogical information. The list shows the state agencies which provide records of vital statistics (births, deaths, and marriages), an agency or private organization which has general information on a variety of questions relating to research, and a supplementary listing of libraries which have especially notable genealogical collections.

In general, requests for information or searches in vital records, if sent to the state agency given here, will be forwarded to the appropriate local or county agency. However, to save time and insure success, it is best to make inquiries directly to the appropriate local agency, should such agency be so indicated in this listing. The fees for searches in these vital records vary widely from state to state, and thus have not been given here. As a general rule, it is best to request information about search procedures and fees *before* requesting the actual search.

Finally be aware of the fact that many states have a separate category of "delayed birth registrations." This category includes births which occurred before birth registrations were required or births which were not registered at the time they occurred for many and varied reasons. If you suspect that the information you seek may fall in this category, be sure to request a special search of this separate registration file.

The libraries and archival repositories, as well as the state agencies for history, listed in this chapter vary widely as to the nature of their collections and procedures for research. A preliminary inquiry or visit may, thus, help you to gain a clearer understanding of what to expect from them when and as your research requirements develop.

This chapter has been included as a general reference list. It will serve as an extremely useful tool for the many novice genealogists who have only a vague idea of how to acquire information concerning vital records. The list below should clear up any questions you may have about exactly where to write for birth and death dates and for marriage records. The following state-by-state list is well worth your attention, especially because the libraries listed under each state are those which are most likely to hold the greatest amount of genealogical information for each state. It should also be remembered that many states have had their boundary lines altered (see chapter three) since their initial statehood; if you are unsuccessful in obtaining the data you need from one state, be sure to write to the bureaus of vital statistics of neighboring states. Just as when you are seeking information from a court house, from a relative, or from a friend, it is wise to remember the importance of making your inquiry as precise as possible.

ALABAMA

For birth and death records since 1 January 1908, contact:

Bureau of Vital Statistics
State Department of Public Health
Montgomery, Alabama 36104

For marriage records since August 1936, contact:

Bureau of Vital Statistics
State Department of Public Health
Montgomery, Alabama 36105

For marriage records contact:
Probate Judge in county where license was issued

For general information on genealogical archives and records, contact:
Alabama Department of Archives and History
624 Washington Avenue
Montgomery, Alabama 36104

Other libraries include:
Mobile Public Library
Special Collections Division
701 Government Street
Mobile, Alabama 36602

ALASKA

For birth and death records, since 1931, contact:
Bureau of Vital Statistics
Department of Health and Welfare
Pouch "H"
Juneau, Alaska 99801

For marriage records, since 1913, contact:
Bureau of Vital Statistics
Department of Health and Welfare
Pouch "H"
Juneau, Alaska 99801

For general information on genealogical archives and records, contact:
Alaska Historical Library
Pouch "G"
State Capitol
Juneau, Alaska 99801

Other libraries include:
Alaska State Museum
Pouch "F.M."
Subport
Juneau, Alaska 99801

ARIZONA

For birth and death records, since 1 July 1909, contact:*
Division of Vital Statistics
State Department of Health
P. O. Box 6820
Phoenix, Arizona 85005

For marriage records, contact:
Clerk of Superior Court in county where license was issued

For general information on genealogical archives and records, contact:
Arizona State Department of Library and Archives
Third Floor
State Capitol
Phoenix, Arizona 85007

Other library sources include:
Walter C. Cox Foundation Library
1701 North Eleventh Street
P. O. Box 5167
Tucson, Arizona 85703

ARKANSAS

For birth and death records, since 1 February 1914,† contact:
Bureau of Vital Statistics
State Department of Health
Little Rock, Arkansas 72201

For marriage records, since 1917,‡ contact:
Bureau of Vital Statistics
State Department of Health
Little Rock, Arkansas 72201

* State office also has abstracts of records before that date.

† State office also has some records for Little Rock and Fort Smith from 1881.

‡ For records before 1917, contact County Clerk in county where license was issued.

For general information on genealogical archives and records, contact:

Arkansas History Commission
Old State House
Little Rock, Arkansas 72201

Other libraries include:

Little Rock Public Library
700 Louisiana Street
Little Rock, Arkansas 72201 *or*
Pine Bluff and Jefferson County
Public Library
200 East Eighth Avenue
Pine Bluff, Arkansas 71601

CALIFORNIA

For birth and death records, since 1 July 1900, contact:*

Bureau of Vital statistics
State Department of Public Health
1927 Thirteenth Street
Sacramento, California 95814

For marriage records, contact:

Bureau of Vital Statistics
State Department of Public Health
744 P Street
Sacramento, California 95814

For general information on genealogical archives and records, contact:

California Historical Society
2090 Jackson Street
San Francisco, California 94109 *or*
Conference of California Historical Societies
University of the Pacific
Stockton, California 95204

* For records before that date, contact County Recorder in county where birth or death occurred.

Other libraries include:

- Los Angeles Public Library, History Department
  Genealogy Room
  630 West Fifth Street
  Los Angeles, California 90017
- Pasadena Public Library
  185 East Walnut Street
  Pasadena, California 91101
- Pomona Public Library
  625 South Garey Avenue
  P. O. Box 2271
  Pomona, California 91766
- California State Library
  California Collection
  Library-Courts Building
  P. O. Box 2037
  Sacramento, California 95809
- San Diego Public Library
  820 E Street
  San Diego, California 92101
- San Francisco Public Library
  Department of Rare Books and Special Collections
  Civic Center
  San Francisco, California 94102

COLORADO

For birth and death records, since 1 January 1907, contact:*

Records and Statistics Section
Colorado Department of Health
4210 East Eleventh Avenue
Denver, Colorado 80220

For marriage records, contact:

Records and Statistics Section
Colorado Department of Health

* For records before that date, contact Registrar in county where birth or death occurred.

4210 East Eleventh Avenue
Denver, Colorado 80203

Other libraries include:

- Colorado State Archives
  1530 Sherman
  Denver, Colorado 80203
- Denver Public Library
  1357 Broadway
  Denver, Colorado 80203
- Pikes Peak Regional District Library
  Reference Department
  20 West Kiowa Street
  Colorado Springs, Colorado 80902

CONNECTICUT

For birth and death records since 1 July 1897, contact:*
Public Health Statistics Section
State Department of Health
79 Elm Street
Hartford, Connecticut 06115

For marriage records since 1 July 1897,† contact:
Public Health Statistics Section
State Department of Health
79 Elm Street
Hartford, Connecticut 06115

For general information on genealogical archives and records, contact:
Connecticut Historical Society and Library
1 Elizabeth Street
Hartford, Connecticut 06105 *or*
Connecticut League of Historical Studies

* For records before that date, contact Registrar of Vital Statistics in town or city where birth or death occurred.

† For records before that date, contact Registrar of Vital Statistics in place where license was issued.

114 Whitney Avenue
New Haven, Connecticut 06510

Other libraries include:

- Greenwich Library
  101 West Putnam Avenue
  Greenwich, Connecticut 06830
- Connecticut State Library
  231 Capitol Avenue
  Hartford, Connecticut 06115
- Godfrey Memorial Library
  134 Newfield Street
  Middletown, Connecticut 06457
- New Canaan Historical Society Library
  13 Oenoke Ridge
  New Canaan, Connecticut 06480
- New Haven Colony Historical Society Library
  114 Whitney Avenue
  New Haven, Connecticut 06510
- New London County Historical Society Library
  11 Blinman Street
  New London, Connecticut 06320
- Cyrenium H. Booth Memorial Library
  Newton, Connecticut 06470
- Otis Library
  261 Main Street
  Box 1158
  Norwich, Connecticut 06360
- West Hartford Public Library
  20 East Main Street
  West Hartford, Connecticut 06107

DELAWARE

For birth and death records since 1881 and between 1861-1863, contact:

Bureau of Vital Statistics
State Board of Health

State Health Building
Dover, Delaware 19901

For marriage records, contact:
Bureau of Vital Statistics
Division of Physical Health
Department of Health and Social Services
State Health Building
Dover, Delaware 19901

For general information on genealogical archives and records, contact:
Public Archives Commission
Hall of Records
Dover, Delaware 19901 *or*
Historical Society of Delaware
Sixth and Market Streets
Wilmington, Delaware 19801

Other libraries include:
Wilmington Institute Free Library
Tenth and Market Streets
Wilmington, Delaware 19081

FLORIDA

For birth and death records since January 1917 (and some before), contact:
Bureau of Vital Statistics
State Board of Health
P. O. Box 210
Jacksonville, Florida 32201

For marriage records since 6 June 1917, contact:*
Bureau of Vital Statistics
State Board of Health
P. O. Box 210
Jacksonville, Florida 32201

* For records before that date, contact County Judge in county where license was issued.

For general information on genealogical archives and records, contact:

Florida Board of Archives and History
401 East Gaines Street
Tallahassee, Florida 32301 *or*
Florida Historical Studies
University of South Florida Library
Tampa, Florida 33620

Other libraries include:

- Jacksonville Public Library System
  122 North Ocean Street
  Jacksonville, Florida 32202
- Miami Public Library
  1 Biscayne Blvd. North
  Miami, Florida 33132
- Albertson Public Library
  165 East Central Blvd.
  Orlando, Florida 32801
- Florida State Library
  Supreme Court Building
  Tallahassee, Florida 32304
- Palm Beach County Historical Society Library
  Whitehall Way
  Palm Beach, Florida 33480
- St. Augustine Historical Society Library
  271 Charlotte Street
  St. Augustine, Florida 32084

GEORGIA

For birth and death records since 1 January 1919, contact:*

Vital Records Service
State Department of Public Health
47 Trinity Avenue, S.W.
Atlanta, Georgia 30334

* For records before that date in Atlanta or Savannah, contact County Health Department.

For marriage records, write:
Vital Records Service
State Department of Public Health
47 Trinity Avenue, S.W.
Atlanta, Georgia 30334

For general information on genealogical archives and records, contact:
Georgia Department of Archives and History
330 Capital Avenue, S.E.
Atlanta, Georgia 30334 *or*
Georgia Historical Commission
116 Mitchell Street, S.W.
Atlanta, Georgia 30303

Other libraries include:
- Georgia State Library
301 State Judicial Building
Capital Hill Station
Atlanta, Georgia 30334
- Atlanta Public Library
Reference Department
126 Carnegie Way
Atlanta, Georgia 30303
- Georgia Historical Society Library
501 Whitaker Street
Savannah, Georgia 31401

HAWAII

For birth and death records, since 1853, contact:
Research and Statistics Office
State Department of Health
P. O. Box 3378
Honolulu, Hawaii 96801

For marriage records, contact:
Research and Statistics Office
State Department of Health

P. O. Box 3378
Honolulu, Hawaii 96803

For general information on genealogical archives and records, contact:

Hawaiian Historical Society
560 Kawaiahao Street
Honolulu, Hawaii 96803

Other libraries include:

Public Archives Library
Iolani Palace Grounds
Honolulu, Hawaii 96813

IDAHO

For birth and death records since 1911, contact:*

Bureau of Vital Statistics
State Department of Health
Boise, Idaho 83701

For marriage records since 1947,† contact:

Bureau of Vital Statistics
State Department of Health
Boise, Idaho 83701

For general information on genealogical archives and records, write:

Idaho State Historical Society and Library
610 North Julia Davis Drive
Boise, Idaho 83706

ILLINOIS

For birth and death records since 1 January 1916,‡ contact:

* For records between 1907-1911, contact County Recorder in county where birth or death occurred.

† For records before that date, contact County Recorder in county where license was issued.

‡ For records before that date contact County Clerk in county where birth or death occurred.

Bureau of Statistics
State Department of Public Health
Springfield, Illinois 62706

For marriage records since 1 January 1962, contact:*
Bureau of Statistics
State Department of Public Health
Springfield, Illinois 62706

For general information on genealogical archives and records, contact:
Illinois State Historical Society and Library
Centennial Building
Springfield, Illinois 62706

Other libraries include:
Newberry Library
60 West Walton
Chicago, Illinois 60610

INDIANA

For birth and death records since 1 October 1907 and 1900 respectively,† contact:
Division of Vital Records
State Board of Health
1330 West Michigan Street
Indianapolis, Indiana 46206

For marriage records, contact:
Division of Vital Records
State Board of Health
1330 West Michigan Street
Indianapolis, Indiana 46206

For general information on genealogical archives and records, contact:
Indiana Historical Society and Library

* For records before that date, contact County Clerk in county where license was issued.

† For records before those dates, contact Health Officer in town or county where birth and death occurred.

140 North Senate Avenue
Indianapolis, Indiana 46204 *or*
Indiana Historical Bureau
State Library and Historical Building
Indianapolis, Indiana 46204

Other libraries include:

- Public Library of Fort Wayne and Allen County
  900 Webster Street
  Fort Wayne, Indiana 46802
- Franklin Public Library
  Madison and Home Avenue
  Franklin, Indiana 46131
- Indianapolis Marion County Public Library
  40 East St. Clair Street
  Indianapolis, Indiana 46204
- Emeline Fairbanks Memorial Library
  222 North Seventh Street
  Terre Haute, Indiana 47807

IOWA

For birth and death records since 1 July 1880, contact:
Division of Records and Statistics
State Department of Health
Des Moines, Iowa 50319

For marriage records, contact:
Division of Records and Statistics
State Department of Health
Des Moines, Iowa 50319

For general information on genealogical archives and records, contact:
State Historical Society of Iowa Library
University of Iowa
Iowa City, Iowa 52240

Other libraries include:

- Iowa Historical and Genealogical Library
  Department of History and Archives

East Twelfth Street and Grand Avenue
Des Moines, Iowa 50319

- Oskaloosa Public Library
South Market and Second Avenue West
Oskaloosa, Iowa 52577
- Sioux City Public Library
705 Sixth Street
Sioux City, Iowa 55105
- Waterloo Public Library
Fifth and Mulberry Streets
Waterloo, Iowa 50703
- Gibson Memorial Library
310 North Maple
Creston, Iowa 50801

KANSAS

For birth and death records since 1 July 1911, contact:*
Division of Vital Statistics
State Department of Health
Topeka, Kansas 66612

For marriage records since May 1913,† contact:
Division of Vital Statistics
State Department of Health
Topeka, Kansas 66612

For general information on genealogical archives and records, contact:
Kansas State Historical Society and Library
120 West Tenth Street
Topeka, Kansas 66612

Other libraries include:
Kansas City Public Library
625 Minnesota Avenue

* For records before that date, contact County Clerk in county where birth or death occurred.

† For records before that date, contact Probate Judge in county where license was issued.

Kansas City, Kansas 66101 *or*
Wichita Public Library
223 South Main Street
Wichita, Kansas 67202

KENTUCKY

For birth and death records since 1 January 1911 (and before in Louisville and Lexington), contact:

Office of Vital Statistics
State Department of Health
275 East Main Street
Frankfort, Kentucky 40601

For marriage records since 1 July 1958, contact:*

Office of Vital Statistics
State Department of Health
275 East Main Street
Frankfort, Kentucky 40601

For general information on genealogical archives and records, contact:

Kentucky Historical Society
Old State House
P. O. Box H
Frankfort, Kentucky 40601

Other libraries include:

- Filson Club Library
  118 West Breckenridge Street
  Louisville, Kentucky 40203
- Henderson Public Library
  101 South Main Street
  Henderson, Kentucky 42420
- John Fox Memorial Library
  Duncan Tavern Street
  Paris, Kentucky 40361

* For records before that date, contact Clerk of Court in county where license was issued.

- Lexington Public Library
  251 West Second Street
  Lexington, Kentucky 40361
- Louisville Free Public Library
  Fourth and York Streets
  Louisville, Kentucky 40203

LOUISIANA

For birth and death records since 1 July 1914, contact:

Division of Public Health Statistics
State Board of Health
P. O. Box 60630
New Orleans, Louisiana 70160

For birth and death records since 1790 and 1803 respectively in the City of New Orleans only, contact:

Bureau of Vital Statistics
City Health Department
1W03 City Hall, Civic Center
New Orleans, Louisiana 70112

For marriage records in the City of New Orleans only, contact:

Bureau of Vital Statistics
City Health Department
1WO3 City Hall, Civic Center
New Orleans, Louisiana 70112

For general information on genealogical archives and records, contact:

Louisiana Historical Association
Box 44222– Capital Station
Baton Rouge, Louisiana 70804

Other libraries include:

- Louisiana State Library
  State Capital Grounds
  760 North Third Street
  Baton Rouge, Louisiana 70821

- East Baton Rouge Parish Library
  700 Laurel Street
  Baton Rouge, Louisiana 70802
- Ouchita Parish Public Library
  1800 Stubbs Avenue
  Monroe, Louisiana 71201
- Shreve Memorial Library
  400 Edwards Street
  P. O. Box 1523
  Shreveport, Louisiana 71102

MAINE

For birth and death records since 1892, contact:*
Office of Vital Statistics
State Department of Health and Welfare
State House
Augusta, Maine 04330

For marriage records, contact:
Office of Vital Statistics
State Department of Health and Welfare
State House
Augusta, Maine 04330

For general information on genealogical archives and records, contact:
Maine Historical Society
485 Congress Street
Portland, Maine 04111

Other libraries include:
Maine State Library and Archives
State House
Augusta, Maine 04330 *or*
Bangor Public Library
145 Harlow Street
Bangor, Maine 04401

* For records before that date, contact Town Clerk where birth or death occurred.

MARYLAND

For birth and death records since 1898, contact:

Division of Vital Records
State Department of Health
State Office Building
301 West Preston Street
Baltimore, Maryland 21201

For birth and death records since 1875 in the city of Baltimore only, write:

Bureau of Vital Records
City Health Department
Municipal Office Building
Baltimore, Maryland 21202

For marriage records since 1 June 1952, contact:*

Division of Vital Records
State Department of Health and Mental Hygiene
State Office Building
301 West Preston Street
Baltimore, Maryland 21201

For general information on genealogical archives and records, contact:

Maryland Historical Society
201 West Monument Street
Baltimore, Maryland 21201

Other libraries include:

- Maryland Hall of Records Commission Library
  College Avenue and St. John's Street
  Annapolis, Maryland 21401
- Maryland State Library

* For records before that date, contact Clerk of Circuit Court in county where license was issued or clerk of court of Common Pleas in Baltimore.

Court of Appeals Building
P. O. Box 191
Annapolis, Maryland 21404

- Enoch Pratt Free Library, Peabody Department
17 East Mount Vernon Place
Baltimore, Maryland 21202

MASSACHUSETTS

For birth and death records since 1841, contact:*
Registrar of Vital Statistics
272 State House
Boston, Massachusetts 02133

For birth and death records since 1639 in the City of Boston only, contact:
City Registrar
Registry Division
Health Department
Room 705, City Hall Annex
Boston, Massachusetts 02133

For marriage records since 1841, contact:
Registrar of Vital Statistics
272 State House
Boston, Massachusetts 02133

For general information on genealogical archives and records, contact:
Massachusetts Historical Society
1154 Boylston Street
Boston, Massachusetts 02115 *or*
Bay State Historical League
Room 51
The State House
Boston, Massachusetts 02133

Other libraries include:
- The Jones Library

* For records before that date, contact Town Clerk in place where birth or death occurred.

Amity Street
Amherst, Massachusetts 01002

- Beverly Historical Society
  Charles W. Galloupe Memorial Library
  117 Cabot Street
  Beverly, Massachusetts 01915
- Boston Public Library
  Copley Square
  P. O. Box 286
  Boston, Massachusetts 02117
- Massachusetts State Library
  State House
  Boston, Massachusetts 02133
- New England Historic Genealogical Society Library
  101 Newbury Street
  Boston, Massachusetts 02116
- Cambridge Public Library
  449 Broadway
  Cambridge, Massachusetts 02138
- Haverhill Public Library
  99 Main Street
  Haverhill, Massachusetts 01830
- Lynn Public Library
  5 North Common Street
  Lynn, Massachusetts 01902
- Berkshire Athenaeum
  44 Bank Row
  Pittsfield, Massachusetts 01201
- Essex Institute
  James Duncan Phillips Library
  132-134 Essex Street
  Salem, Massachusetts 01970
- Westfield Athenaeum
  6 Elm Street
  Westfield, Massachusetts 01085
- American Antiquarian Society Library
  Salisbury Street and Park Avenue
  Worcester, Massachusetts 01609

MICHIGAN

For birth and death records since 1867, contact:

Vital Records Section
Michigan Department of Health
3500 North Logan Street
Lansing, Michigan 48914

For marriage records since 1867, contact:

Vital Records Section
Michigan Department of Health
3500 North Logan Street
Lansing, Michigan 48914

For general information on genealogical archives and records, contact:

Historical Society of Michigan
2117 Washtenaw Avenue
Ann Arbor, Michigan 48104

Other libraries include:

- Detroit Public Library
  5201 Woodward Avenue
  Detroit, Michigan 48202
- Grand Rapids Public Library
  Michigan Genealogy Department
  Library Plaza, N.E.
  Grand Rapids, Michigan 49502
- Herrick Public Library
  300 River Avenue
  Holland, Michigan 49423
- State Archives and Library
  Michigan Historical Commission
  3405 North Logan Street
  Lansing, Michigan 49818
- Michigan State Library
  735 East Michigan Avenue
  Lansing, Michigan 48913

MINNESOTA

For birth and death records since January 1900, contact:
Section of Vital Statistics
State Department of Health
350 State Office Building
St. Paul, Minnesota 55101

For marriage records, contact:
Section of Vital Statistics
State Department of Health
717 Delaware Street, S.E.
Minneapolis, Minnesota 55440

For general information on genealogical archives and records, contact:
Minnesota Historical Society and Library
690 Cedar Street
St. Paul, Minnesota 55101

Other libraries include:
Minneapolis Public Library
300 Nicollet Mall
Minneapolis, Minnesota 55401 *or*
St. Paul Public Library
90 West Fourth Street
St. Paul, Minnesota 55102

MISSISSIPPI

For birth and death records since 1 November 1912, contact:
Division of Public Health Statistics
State Board of Health
P. O. Box 1700
Jackson, Mississippi, 39205

For marriage records since January 1926, contact:*

* For records before that date, contact Circuit Clerk in county where license was issued.

Vital Records Registration Unit
State Board of Health
P. O. Box 1700
Jackson, Mississippi 39205

For general information on genealogical archives and records, contact:

Mississippi State Department of Archives and History
P. O. Box 571
War Memorial Building
120 North State Street
Jackson, Mississippi 39201

Other libraries include:

Evans Memorial Library
Aberdeen, Mississippi 39730 *or*
Lauren Rogers Library and Museum of Art
Fifth Avenue and Seventh Street
P. O. Box 1108
Laurel, Mississippi 39440

MISSOURI

For birth and death records since January 1910, contact:*

Vital Records
Division of Health
State Department of Public Health and Welfare
Jefferson City, Missouri 65101

For marriage records since July 1948,† contact:

Vital Records
Division of Health
State Department of Public Health and Welfare
Jefferson City, Missouri 65101

For general information on genealogical archives and records, contact:

State Historical Society of Missouri

* For records in St. Louis or Kansas City Health Department.

† For records before that date, contact Recorder of Deeds in county where license was issued.

University Library Building
Hitt and Lowry Streets
Columbia, Missouri 55201

Other libraries include:

- Kansas City Public Library
  311 East Twelfth Street
  Kansas City, Missouri 64152
- Concordia Historical Institute
  301 Demun Avenue
  St. Louis, Missouri 63105
- St. Louis Public Library
  1031 Olive Street
  St. Louis, Missouri 63103

MONTANA

For birth and death records since 1907, contact:
Division of Records and Statistics
State Department of Health
Helena, Montana 59601

For marriage records since July 1943, contact:*
Division of Records and Statistics
State Department of Health
Helena, Montana 59601

For general information on genealogical archives and records, contact:
Montana Historical Society
225 North Roberts Street
Helena, Montana 59601

Other libraries include:

- Parmly Billings Memorial Library
  Montana and 29th Streets
  Billings, Montana 59101
- Butte Free Public Library
  106 West Broadway Street

* For records before that date, contact Clerk of District Court where license was issued.

Butte, Montana 59701

- Missoula Public Library
  Pine and Pattee Streets
  Missoula, Montana 59801

NEBRASKA

For birth and death records, contact:

Bureau of Vital Statistics
State Department of Health
State Capitol
Lincoln, Nebraska 68509

For marriage records since January 1909, contact:*

Bureau of Vital Statistics
State Department of Health
State Capitol
Lincoln, Nebraska 68509

For general information on genealogical archives and records, contact:

Nebraska State Historical Society
1500 R Street
Lincoln, Nebraska 68508

Other libraries include:

- Alliance Public Library
  202 West Fourth Street
  Alliance, Nebraska 69301
- Grand Island Public Library
  321 West Second Street
  Grand Island, Nebraska 68801
- Lincoln Public Library
  136 South Fourteenth Street
  Lincoln, Nebraska 68508
- Omaha Public Library
  Nineteenth and Harney Streets
  Omaha, Nebraska 68102

* For records before that date, contact County Court where license was issued.

NEVADA

For birth and death records since 1 July 1911, contact:*
Department of Health, Welfare, and Rehabilitation
Division of Health
Section of Vital Statistics
Carson City, Nevada 89701

For marriage records, contact:
County Recorder in county where license was issued

For general information on genealogical archives and records, contact:
Nevada State Historical Society and Library
P. O. Box 1129
Reno, Nevada 89504

Other libraries include:
City Library of Las Vegas
400 East Mesquite Avenue
Las Vegas, Nevada 89101

NEW HAMPSHIRE

For birth and death records, contact:
Department of Health and Welfare
Division of Public Health
Bureau of Vital Statistics
61 South Spring Street
Concord, New Hampshire 03301

For marriage records, contact:
Department of Health and Welfare
Division of Public Health
Bureau of Vital Statistics
61 South Spring Street
Concord, New Hampshire 03301

* For records before that date, contact County Recorder in county where birth or death occurred.

For general information on genealogical archives and records, contact:

New Hampshire Historical Society and Library
30 Park Street
Concord, New Hampshire 03301

Other libraries include:

New Hampshire State Library
20 Park Street
Concord, New Hampshire 03302 *or*
City Library
405 Pine Street
Manchester, New Hampshire 03104

NEW JERSEY

For birth and death records since June 1878, contact:

State Department of Health
Bureau of Vital Statistics
P. O. Box 1540
Trenton, New Jersey 08625

For marriage records since June 1878, contact:

State Department of Health
Bureau of Vital Statistics
P. O. Box 1540
Trenton, New Jersey 08625

For any vital records before 1878, contact:

Archives and History Bureau
State Library Division
State Department of Education
Trenton, New Jersey 08625

For general information on genealogical archives and records, contact:

New Jersey Historical Society
230 Broadway
Newark, New Jersey 07104

Other libraries include:

- Free Public Library
  Illinois and Pacific Avenues
  Atlantic City, New Jersey 08401
- Monmouth County Historical Association
  Museum and Library
  70 Court Street
  Freehold, New Jersey 07728
- Morristown Library
  Miller Road and South Street
  Morristown, New Jersey 07960
- Plainfield Public Library
  Eighth Street and Park Avenue
  Plainfield, New Jersey 07060
- New Jersey State Library
  Archives and History Bureau
  185 West State Street
  Trenton, New Jersey 08625

NEW MEXICO

For birth and death records, contact:

Vital Records
New Mexico Health and Social Services Department
PERA Building
Room 118
Santa Fe, New Mexico 87501

For marriage records, contact:

County Clerk in county where license was issued

For general information on genealogical archives and records, contact:

Museum of New Mexico
P. O. Box 2087
Santa Fe, New Mexico 87501

Other libraries include:

New Mexico State Library Commission

301 Don Gasper
Santa Fe, New Mexico 87051 *or*
Albuquerque Public Library
423 East Central Avenue
Albuquerque, New Mexico 87101

NEW YORK

For birth and death records since 1880, contact:*
Bureau of Vital Records
State Department of Health
Albany, New York 12208

For birth and death records in Borough of Bronx, City of New York only, contact:
Bureau of Records and Statistics
Department of Health of New York City
1826 Arthur Avenue
Bronx, New York 10457

For birth and death records in Borough of Brooklyn, City of New York only, contact:
County Clerk, Kings County
Historical Division
260 Adams Street
Brooklyn, New York 11201 *or*
Bureau of Records and Statistics
Department of Health of New York City
295 Flatbush Avenue Extension
Brooklyn, New York 11201

For birth and death records in Borough of Manhattan, City of New York only, contact:
Bureau of Records and Statistics
Department of Health of New York City
125 Worth Street
New York, New York 10013

* For records before 1880 and before 1914 in Albany, Buffalo, and Yonkers, contact Registrar of Vital Statistics in city where birth or death occurred.

For birth and death records in the Borough of Queens, City of New York only, contact:
Bureau of Records and Statistics
Department of Health of New York City
90-37 Parsons Blvd.
Jamaica, New York 11432

For birth and death records in the Borough of Richmond, City of New York only, contact:
Bureau of Records and Statistics
Department of Health of New York City
51 Stuyvesant Place
St. George, Staten Island
New York 10301

For marriage records, contact:
Bureau of Vital Records
State Department of Health
Albany, New York 12208

For marriage records in the Borough of the Bronx, City of New York only, contact:
Office of City Clerk
1780 Grand Concourse
Bronx, New York 11201

For marriage records in the Borough of Brooklyn, City of New York only, contact:
Office of City Clerk
Municipal Building
Brooklyn, New York 11201

For marriage records in the Borough of Manhattan, City of New York only, contact:
Office of City Clerk
Municipal Building
New York, New York 10007

For marriage records in the Borough of Queens, City of New York only, contact:
Office of City Clerk
120-55 Queens Blvd.

Borough Hall Station
Jamaica, New York 11424

For marriage records in the Borough of Richmond, City of New York only, contact:

Office of City Clerk
Borough Hall
St. George, Staten Island
New York 10301

For general information on genealogical archives and records, contact:

New York State Historical Association
Lake Road
Cooperstown, New York 13326

Other libraries include:

- Long Island Historical Society and Library
  128 Pierrepont Street
  Brooklyn, New York 11201
- Newburgh Free Library
  100 Grand Street
  Newburgh, New York 12550
- Holland Society of New York, Library
  15 William Street
  New York, New York 10005
- New York Genealogical and Biographical Society Library
  122-126 East 58th Street
  New York, New York 10022
- The New York Historical Society Library
  170 Central Park West
  New York, New York 10024
- New York Public Library
  American History and Genealogy Division
  Fifth Avenue and 42nd Street
  New York, New York 10018
- Smithtown Public Library
  East Main Street
  Smithtown, New York 11787

- Syracuse Public Library
  335 Montgomery Street
  Syracuse, New York 13202

NORTH CAROLINA

For birth and death records since 1 October 1913, contact:
Public Health Statistics Section
State Board of Health
P. O. Box 2091
Raleigh, North Carolina 27602

For marriage records since 1 January 1962, contact:*
Public Health Statistics Section
State Board of Health
P. O. Box 2091
Raleigh, North Carolina 27602

For general information on genealogical archives and records, contact:
State Department of Archives and History
P. O. Box 1881
Raleigh, North Carolina 27601

Other libraries include:

- Pack Memorial Public Library
  Pack Square
  Ashville, North Carolina 28801
- North Carolina State Library
  Salisbury and Edenton Streets
  P. O. Box 2889
  Raleigh, North Carolina
- Smathers National Memorial Collections of Genealogical Records
  Haywood County Public Library
  Boyd Avenue
  Waynesville, North Carolina 28786

* For records before that date, contact Registrar of Deeds in county where marriage was performed.

NORTH DAKOTA

For birth and death records since 1 July 1893, contact:

Division of Vital Statistics
State Department of Health
Bismarck, North Dakota 58501

For marriage records, contact:

Division of Vital Statistics
State Department of Health
Bismarck, North Dakota 58501

For general information on genealogical archives and records, contact:

State Historical Society of North Dakota
Liberty Memorial Building
Bismarck, North Dakota 58501

Other libraries include:

- North Dakota State Library Commission
  High 83
  Bismarck, North Dakota 58501
- Fargo Public Library
  120 Third Street North
  Fargo, North Dakota 58102
- Grand Forks Public Library
  423 First Avenue North
  Grand Forks, North Dakota 58201
- Minot Public Library
  516 Second Avenue, S.W.
  Minot, North Dakota 58701

OHIO

For birth and death records since 20 December 1908, contact:*

Division of Vital Statistics
State Department of Health

* For records before that date, contact Probate Court in county where birth or death occurred.

G-20 State Department Building
Columbus, Ohio 43215

For marriage records, contact:
Division of Vital Statistics
State Department of Health
G-20 State Department Building
Columbus, Ohio 43215

For general information on genealogical archives and records, contact:
Ohio Historical Society
North High Street and 15th Avenue
Columbus, Ohio 43210

Other libraries include:

- Public Library of Cincinnati and Hamilton County
  Eighth and Vine Streets
  Cincinnati, Ohio 45202
- Cleveland Public Library
  History, Biography, and Travel Department
  325 Superior Avenue
  Cleveland, Ohio 44114
- Western Reserve Historical Society Library
  10825 East Blvd.
  Cleveland, Ohio 44106
- Dayton and Montgomery County Library
  215 East Third Street
  Dayton, Ohio 45402
- Rutherford B. Hayes Library
  1337 Hayes Avenue
  Freemont, Ohio 43420
- Free Public Library
  1320 First Avenue
  Middletown, Ohio 45042
- Toledo Public Library
  325 Michigan Street
  Toledo, Ohio 43624

OKLAHOMA

For birth and death records since October 1908, contact:
Division of Statistics
State Department of Health
3400 North Eastern
Oklahoma City, Oklahoma 73105

For marriage records, contact:
Clerk of Court in county where license was issued

For general information on genealogical archives and records, contact:
Oklahoma Historical Society
Historical Building
Oklahoma City, Oklahoma 73105

Other libraries include:
Oklahoma State Library
109 Capitol
Oklahoma City, Oklahoma 73105 *or*
Tulsa City-County Library
400 Civic Center
Tulsa, Oklahoma 74103

OREGON

For birth and death records, since July 1903, contact:*
Vital Statistics Section
State Board of Health
P. O. Box 231
Portland, Oregon 97207

For marriage records since January 1970,† contact:
Vital Statistics Section
State Board of Health

* For records before 1915 in Portland, contact Bureau of Health, Portland, Oregon 97107.

† For records before that date, contact County Clerk in county where license was issued.

P. O. Box 231
Portland, Oregon 97207

For general information on genealogical archives and records contact:

Oregon Historical Society
1230 S.W. Park Avenue
Portland, Oregon 97205

Other libraries include:

Multnamah County Library
801 S.W. 10th Street
Portland, Oregon 97205 *or*
Oregon State Archives and Library
State Library Building
Salem, Oregon 97310

PENNSYLVANIA

For birth and death records since 1 January 1906, contact:*

Division of Vital Statistics
State Department of Health
Health and Welfare Building
P. O. Box 90
Harrisburg, Pennsylvania 17120

For marriage records, contact:

Division of Vital Statistics
State Department of Health
Health and Welfare Building
P. O. Box 90
Harrisburg, Pennsylvania 17120

For general information on genealogical archives and records, contact:

Pennsylvania Historical and Museum Commission
William Penn Memorial Museum

* For records before that date, contact Registrar of Wills, Orphans Court, in the county where the birth or death occurred.

P. O. Box 1026
Harrisburg, Pennsylvania 17108

Other libraries include:
Pennsylvania State Library
Genealogy Section
Educational Building
P. O. Box 1601
Harrisburg, Pennsylvania 17126 *or*
City History Society of Pennsylvania Library
4237 Sansom Street
Philadelphia, Pennsylvania 19104

RHODE ISLAND

For birth and death records since 1853 contact:*
Division of Vital Statistics
State Department of Health
State Office Building
Room 351
Providence, Rhode Island 02903

For marriage records since 1853,† contact:
Division of Vital Statistics
State Department of Health
State Office Building
Room 353
Providence, Rhode Island 02903

For general information on genealogical archives and records, contact:
Rhode Island Historical Society
52 Powell Street
Providence, Rhode Island 02903

Other libraries include:
Providence Public Library

* For records before that date, contact town clerk in town where birth or death occurred.

† For records before that date, contact Town Clerk in town where marriage was performed.

229 Washington Street
Providence, Rhode Island 02903 *or*
Westerly Public Library
Broad Street
P. O. Box 356
Westerly, Rhode Island 02891

SOUTH CAROLINA

For birth and death records since 1 January 1915, contact:*
Bureau of Vital Statistics
State Board of Health
Sims Building
Columbia, South Carolina 29201

For marriage records since 1 July 1950,† contact:
Bureau of Vital Statistics
State Board of Health
Sims Building
Columbia, South Carolina 29201

For general information on genealogical archives and records, contact:
South Carolina Department of Archives and History
1430 Senate Street
Columbia, South Carolina 29201

Other libraries include:
Free Library
404 King Street
Charleston, South Carolina 29407

SOUTH DAKOTA

For birth and death records, contact:
Division of Public Health Statistics

* For earlier records in Charleston, Newberry City, or Florence City, contact the respective County Health Department.
† For records between 1911-1950, contact Probate Judge in County where license was issued.

State Department of Health
Pierre, South Dakota 57501

For marriage records since 1 July 1905, contact:*
Division of Public Health Statistics
State Department of Health
Pierre, South Dakota 57501

For general information on genealogical archives and records, contact:
South Dakota Historical Society and Library
Memorial Building
Pierre, South Dakota 57501

Other libraries include:
Alexander Mitchell Public Library
21 Sixth Avenue, S.E.
Aberdeen, South Dakota 57401 *or*
Carnegie Free Public Library
Tenth and Dakota Streets
Sioux Falls, South Dakota 57102

TENNESSEE

For birth and death records since 1 January 1914,† contact:
Division of Vital Statistics
State Department of Public Health
Cordell Hull Building
Nashville, Tennessee 37219

For marriage records since July 1945,‡ contact:
Division of Vital Statistics
State Department of Public Health

* For records before that date contact Clerk of Courts in county where license was issued.

† State office also has records for Nashville from July 1881, for Knoxville from July 1881, and for Chattanooga from January 1882.

‡ For records before that date, contact County Court Clerk in County where license was issued.

Cordell Hull Building
Nashville, Tennessee 37219

For general information on genealogical archives and records, contact:

Tennessee Historical Commission
State Library and Archives Building
Nashville, Tennessee 37219

Other libraries include:

Chattanooga Public Library
Historical Collections
601 McCallie Avenue
Chattanooga, Tennessee 37402 *or*
Memphis Public Library
Cossitt-Goodwyn Libraries
33 South Front Street
Memphis, Tennessee 38103

TEXAS

For birth and death records, contact:

Bureau of Vital Statistics
State Department of Health
410 East Fifth Street
Austin, Texas 78701

For marriage records, contact:

County Clerk in county where license was issued

For general information on genealogical archives and records, contact:

Texas State Historical Association
Box 8059
University Station
Austin, Texas 78712

Other libraries include:

▪ Jay-Rollins Library
McMurry College

McMurry Station
Abilene, Texas 79605

- Tyrrell Public Library
695 Pearl Street
Beaumont, Texas 77704
- Dallas Public Library
1954 Commerce Street
Dallas, Texas 75201
- Fort Worth Public Library
Ninth and Throckmorton Streets
Fort Worth, Texas 76106
- Houston Public Library
Historical Room
500 McKinney Avenue
Houston, Texas 77002
- San Antonio Public Library
History, Social Science and General Reference Department
210 West Market
San Antonio, Texas 78205

UTAH

For birth and death records since 1905, contact:*
Division of Vital Statistics
Utah State Department of Health
44 Medical Drive
Salt Lake City, Utah 84113

For marriage records, contact:
County Clerk in county where the license was issued

For general information on genealogical archives and records, contact:
Utah State Historical Society and Library
603 East South Temple
Salt Lake City, Utah 84111

* For records between 1890-1904 in Salt Lake City or Ogden contact City Board of Health.

Other libraries include:

Genealogical Society of Jesus Christ of Latter-day Saints and Library
107 South Main Street
Salt Lake City, Utah 84111

VERMONT

For birth and death records, contact:

Secretary of State
Vital Records Department
State House
Montpellier, Vermont 05602

For marriage records since 1857, contact:*

Secretary of State
Vital Records Department
State House
Montpellier, Vermont 05602

For general information on genealogical archives and records, contact:

Vermont Historical Society and Library
State Administration Building
Montpellier, Vermont 05602

Other libraries include:

Bennington Museum and Library
West Main Street
Barrington, Vermont 05201

VIRGINIA

For birth and death records between January 1858-December 1896 and since 4 June 1912,† contact:

* For records before that date, contact Town Clerk in town where license was issued.

† For records between 1896-1911, contact Health Department in place where birth or death occurred.

Bureau of Vital Records and Statistics
State Department of Health
James Madison Building
P. O. Box 1000
Richmond, Virginia 23208

For marriage records since 1853, contact:*
Bureau of Vital Records and Statistics
State Department of Health
James Madison Building
P. O. Box 1000
Richmond, Virginia 23208

For general information on genealogical archives and records, contact:
Virginia Historical Society and Library
428 North Blvd.
P. O. Box 7311
Richmond, Virginia 23221

Other libraries include:

- Jones Memorial Library
434 Rivermont Avenue
Lynchburg, Virginia 24504
- Virginia State Library
Capitol Street
Richmond, Virginia 23219
- College of William and Mary
Earl Gregg Swem Library
Williamsburg, Virginia 23185

WASHINGTON

For birth and death records since 1 July 1907,† contact:
Bureau of Vital Statistics

* For records before that date, contact Court Clerk in place where license was issued.

† For records before that date, contact Auditor in county where birth or death occurred.

State Department of Health
Olympia, Washington 98501

For marriage records since 1 January 1968, contact:*
Bureau of Vital Statistics
Division of Health
Washington State Department of Social and Health Services
Olympia, Washington 98501

For general information on genealogical archives and records, contact:
Washington State Historical Society and Library
315 North Stadium Way
Tacoma, Washington 98403

Other libraries include:
- Everett Public Library
  2700 Hoyt Avenue
  Everett, Washington 98201
- Washington State Library
  Olympia, Washington 98501
- Seattle Public Library
  1000 Fourth Avenue
  Seattle, Washington 98104
- Spokane Public Library
  906 West Main Avenue
  Spokane, Washington 99201

WEST VIRGINIA

For birth and death records, since January 1917,† contact:
Division of Vital Statistics
State Department of Health
State Office Building No. 3
Charleston, West Virginia 25311

* For records before that date, contact Auditor in county where license was issued.

† For records before that date, contact Clerk of County Court in county where birth or death occurred.

For marriage records, contact:
Division of Vital Statistics
State Department of Health
State Office Building No. 3
Charleston, West Virginia 25311

For general information on genealogical archives and records, contact:
West Virginia Department of Archives and History
Room E-400
State Capitol
Charleston, West Virginia 25305

Other libraries include:
West Virginia Historical, Archival, and Genealogical Collection University of West Virginia
Morgantown, West Virginia 26506

WISCONSIN

For birth and death records, contact:
Bureau of Health Statistics
Wisconsin Division of Health
P. O. Box 309
Madison, Wisconsin 53701

For marriage records, contact:
Bureau of Health Statistics
Wisconsin Division of Health
P. O. Box 309
Madison, Wisconsin 53701

For general information on genealogical archives and records, contact:
State Historical Society of Wisconsin
816 State Street
Madison, Wisconsin 53706

Other libraries include:
Milwaukee Public Library

814 West Wisconsin Avenue
Milwaukee, Wisconsin 53233

WYOMING

For birth and death records, contact:

Bureau of Vital Statistics
State Department of Public Health
State Office Building
Cheyenne, Wyoming 82001

For marriage records since May 1941, contact:*

Vital Records Services
Division of Health and Medical Services
State Office Building
Cheyenne, Wyoming 82001

For general information on genealogical archives and records, contact:

Wyoming State Archives and Historical Department
State Office Building
Cheyenne, Wyoming 81001 *or*
Wyoming State Historical Society
State Office Building
Cheyenne, Wyoming 82001

Other libraries include:

Wyoming State Library
Supreme Court Building
Cheyenne, Wyoming 82001 *or*
Wyoming State Library
Supreme Court Building
Cheyenne, Wyoming 82001

* For records before that date, contact County Clerk in County where license was issued.

8

FEDERAL GOVERNMENT RESEARCH SOURCES

Paul C. Larsen

Although the records of the federal government were not intended for genealogical use, they serve today as an extensive reservoir of information from which many researchers have located valuable family material. Virtually everybody living in the United States is listed on the records of one government agency or another. This data can be used most effectively when the researcher understands the type of information contained in these records and how it can be made available to him.

The best source for these records is the National Archives in Washington, D.C. While the records here are most advantageously used by visiting the archives, the staff will attempt to locate information requested by mail. If this latter method is employed, the request should be stated as clearly as possible and it should include as much pertinent information as possible. The address of the National Archives is:

National Archives and Records Service
NNC
Washington, D.C. 20408

Probably the oldest records of this nation date back to her independence and recognize the men who fought to achieve that goal. They are the payrolls of the Continental army, which are used primarily today to establish proof of pedigree for admission to patriotic societies.

While these records are the oldest ones authorized and

maintained by the federal government, there are some thirty-eight censuses taken by individual colonies and states between 1600 and 1789 which can be of value to the genealogist. These records, made at the insistence of the British Board of Trade, were used to administer the affairs of the colonies. They were made under the immediate supervision of colonial governors, by sheriffs, justices of the peace, and other county or town officers.

The official censuses of the United States began in 1790. Information from the schedules taken between 1790 and 1880 is available to the public and can be obtained by writing the address above. The censuses taken between 1890 and 1970 are generally unavailable to the public, but they can be obtained by mailing four dollars to:

U.S. Department of Commerce
Bureau of the Census
Pittsburg, Kansas 66762

Although a great deal of genealogical information is contained in the census, they are neither completely accurate nor are they easily usable for the names are only rarely alphabetically arranged. The material collected in each census is listed below:

1790 CENSUS

- Name of the head of the family.
- Number of free white males over 16 years of age.
- Number of free white males under 16 years of age.
- Number of free white females.
- Number of free black persons.
- Number of slaves.

This census, and the ones before 1805, did not distinguish between family members and individuals in the household. Therefore, it is sometimes misleading when the average number of family members is indicated. This figure may have included the cook, a friend, or even a boarder who just happened to be at the house the same day the census taker stopped to perform his job. During the War of 1812, the British stormed Washington and burned several of the city's buildings. Destroyed in that fire were the 1790 census schedules of Delaware, New Jersey, Virginia, Tennessee, Georgia, and Kentucky.

1800 CENSUS

- Name of the head of the family.
- Number of free white males and females under 10 years of age.
- Number of free white males and females between 10 and 16 years of age.
- Number of free white males and females between 16 and 26 years of age.
- Number of free white males and females between 26 and 44 years of age.
- Number of free white males and females over 45 years of age.
- Number of free black persons.
- Number of slaves.

1810 CENSUS

Same information as contained in the 1800 Census.

1820 CENSUS

- Name of the head of the family.
- Number of free white males and females under 10 years of age.
- Number of free white males between 10 and 16 years of age.
- Number of free white males and females between 16 and 18 years of age.

- Number of free white males and females between 18 and 26 years of age.
- Number of free white males and females between 26 and 45 years of age.
- Number of free white males and females over 45 years of age.
- Number of aliens naturalized.
- Number of persons engaged in agriculture, commerce, and manufacturing.
- Number of free black persons.
- Number of slaves.
- Number of all persons except Indians not taxed.

1830 CENSUS

- Name of the head of the family.
- Number of free white persons, age under 5 to 100.
- Number of persons engaged in various professions.
- City, county, ward, township, town, parish, precinct, or district.
- Names and ages of pensioners from Revolutionary War or military service.
- Number of deaf, dumb, and insane white persons.
- Number of deaf, dumb, and insane black persons.
- Information about schools.
- Number of aliens not naturalized.

1840 CENSUS

- Name of the head of the family.
- City, county, ward, township, parish, precinct, or district.
- Number of free white persons, age under 5 to 100.
- Number of persons engaged in various professions.
- Names and ages of pensioners from Revolutionary War or military service.
- Number of deaf, dumb, and insane white persons.
- Number of deaf, dumb, and insane black persons.

1850 CENSUS

- Name, age, sex and color of each person in household.
- Profession of each person over 15 years of age.
- Value of real estate owned.
- Place of birth, including the name of the state, territory or country.
- Weddings within the past year.
- Listing of individuals who attended school in the past year.
- Value of personal property.

1860 CENSUS

Same information as contained in 1850 Census.

1870 CENSUS

Same information as included in previous two censuses.

1880 CENSUS

- Name, age, sex, and color of each person in household.
- Relationship of each person to the head of the family.
- Marital status of each person in household.
- Place of birth of the mother and father of the person listed in census.

It is apparent from the information included in these schedules that a researcher might be able to piece together not only when and where an ancestor lived, but how that ancestor lived. Should the genealogist find his relative listed in one of these early census records, he might be able to determine if his great-grandfather went to school, what kind of occupation he had, the name of his children, and perhaps even the name of his father and mother. There is no question why genealogists believe these records to be among the most important in their research.

THE MORTALITY CENSUS SCHEDULES

Beginning in 1850, enumerators collected information on individuals who died in the twelve-month period prior to the census. These records, called mortality schedules, were compiled as of the first day of June in each decennial year before 1890, including 1885. In 1918 and 1919 the federal government turned these records over to state libraries and historical societies. A researcher should check first for these records in the appropriate state, and as a secondary source he should query the library of the Daughters of the American Revolution, 1776 D Street, N.W., Washington, D.C. The information available on these schedules is:

- Full name, age, sex, and marital status of individual.
- State, territory, or county of birth.
- Month of death.
- Occupation.
- Cause of death.

THE PENSION RECORDS

There is no issue which has come before the Congress of the United States more times than the right to a pension by a military veteran. Ever since the Continental Congress passed the first pension act in 1776, politicians have been heatedly discussing this federal compensation and receiving claims from their constituents. These claims eventually were taken before Congress where they received a vote. Most of them were granted. The applications number in the millions today, and are divided into seven major series in the National Archives. The divisions are (1) Revolutionary War invalid series; (2) Revolutionary War service series; (3) "Old Wars" series; (4) War of 1812 series; (5) Mexican War series; (6) Civil War and later series; (7) Indian wars series.

Many laws passed by Congress which apply to pension records have affected the kind and the amount of information on the claims. In 1818 a law was passed which required a veteran to prove that he was in actual want. Two years later Congress enacted legislation which required the claimant to include a schedule of his whole estate. This information was often presented in the form of a deed which proved that the soldier had disposed of his property. Pension claims after this date are often filled with genealogical material because of the inclusion of the deed.

After 1828 all surviving soldiers who took part in the Revolutionary War were granted pensions. In 1836 the Widow's Act was passed by which a Revolutionary soldier's widow could claim and receive the soldier's pension. The widow needed to prove her relationship, and the source of this proof is of value to the researcher. She would usually submit her marriage certificate or some other documented proof from town or church records. A file showing that a widow applied for a pension normally includes more information than a veteran's file.

Pension records in each of the series mentioned above, except those for the Mexican War, the Civil War and later, and the Indian wars, are arranged alphabetically by name of veteran. The excepted series are arranged numerically by application or certificate number. All series of pension application files have alphabetically name indexes.

There is also a Remarried Widows Index which is in two parts: one part covers records relating to claims based on service in the War of 1812, the Mexican War, the Indian Wars, and the Regular Establishment before 1861; the other covers records relating to claims based on service in the Civil War and later wars, World War I excepted, and in the Regular Establishment after the Civil War. Both parts are arranged alphabetically by the name of the remarried widow. The card also contains information such as the name of the veteran who was the widow's former husband, the designation of the military or naval unit with which he served, and the file or certificate number.

Another set of records closely associated with the pension applications which include a good deal of genealogical information are the pension payment records. These consist of record books kept by the Pension Office and the Treasury Department, and include the official pay vouchers for invalid pensioners, Revolutionary War pensions, naval and privateer pensioners, and pensioners on the rolls of the Pension Office between 1907 and 1933, not including World War I pensioners. The information on these records includes the name and rank of the pensioner, the name of the state in which the payment was made, the amount of the payment, the nature of any disability, or the date of death.

In searching for a man who was known to have filed a pension application, it is imperative that the researcher know the state from which the man came, and even better, the town or county where the man lived. The reason for this is that many names are duplicated and unless positive identification is made, a long and useless search might occur. It should also be remembered that a man who did not serve in the Regular army may have been eligible for a pension if he had served as a militiaman—even if he served for only one day.

Although the records for the Revolutionary War are far from complete, they do offer a source for locating ancestors who lived at that time, and often this may be the only source available. As the nation became more organized, her records reflected it. The documents listing the men who fought in the Indian and Mexican wars are more complete than those of the Revolution, although they do not offer much more information. During the Civil War the records improved to the extent that the enlisting officer often noted a soldier's birthplace, age, and outline of his full service. The records of the Spanish-American War give the soldier's birthplace, age, next to kin, and outline of full service.

The records of the First World War are kept in St. Louis, Missouri. Although these are not generally available to the public, information from them may be obtained by writing the Office of the Adjutant General in the state from which the man served. In conjunction with this period, the selective service cards which were kept at this time are of great aid to the genealogist. In these cards is listed the birthplace, age, residence, next of kin, and the marital status of every man of draft age in the United States in 1918. Information from these cards can be procured by sending a nominal fee to the Federal Records Center in East Point, Georgia.

THE BOUNTY-LAND RECORDS

Land grants are another form of veterans' benefits by which the government rewards its patriots. Bounty-land warrants, granted to veterans or their heirs on the basis of military service performed between the years 1775 and 1855, were a right to free land in the public domain. Land grants were originally extended to Canadian and Nova Scotian refugees as well as to Americans. Later, land use was restricted and only Americans were eligible for land grants. As in the case of pensions, military records were valuable in establishing claims for bounty-land warrants. The inducement of land grants, which encouraged westward migration, coincided with the passage of early land ordinances.

Americans have always placed a high value on land. During and after the American Revolution many large estates were broken up and sold. Laws of inheritance were changed so that all the children of a family, rather than just the older son, could have a share of the land. The early bounty-land warrants and land ordinances marked the emergence of what is often referred to as the *pioneering spirit* of Americans. The opportunity to explore and settle on undeveloped land presented a challenge that many Americans could not resist. Thus bounty-land warrants were an inducement for many men to serve in the military, as well as a reward for the service. Their influence and effect in changing the physical boundaries of this nation are immeasurable. While Congress had previously granted land to specific individuals, the first public grant is dated 16 September 1776, at which time it was resolved.

> That Congress make provision for granting lands in the following proportions: to the officers and soldiers who shall so engage in the service, and continue therein to the close of the war, or until discharged by Congress, and to the representatives of such officers and soldiers as shall be slain by the enemy:
>
> Such lands to be provided by the United States, and whatever expense shall be necessary to procure such land, the said expense shall be paid and borne by the states in the same proportion as the other expenses of war, viz:
>
> To a colonel, 500 acres; to a lieutenant colonel, 450; to a major, 400; to a captain, 300; to a lieutenant, 200; to an ensign, 150; each non-commissioned officer and soldier, 100.

In a later session of Congress, on 22 October 1787, a specific tract of land was set aside for the purpose of supplying these land grants and curtailing unplanned, piecemeal development. Congress resolved:

> That a million acres of land to be bounded east by the 7th range of townships, south by the land contracted for by the Cutler and Sargent and to extend north as far as the ranges of the townships and westward so far as to include the above quantity, also a tract to be bounded as follows beginning at the mouth of the river Ohio thence up the Mississippi to the river AuVasse, thence up the same until it meets a west line from the mouth of the little Wabash thence easterly with the said West line to the Great Wabash, thence down the same to the Ohio and thence with the Ohio to the place of beginning, be reserved and set aside for the purpose of satisfying the military bounties due to the late Army and that no locations other than for the said bounties be permitted within the said tract until they shall be fully satisfied.

The bounty-land warrant application file comprises documents relating to claims for bounty-land based on an individual's military service. Included in these records is a warrant application, a veteran's discharge certificate to substantiate his claim, and a record of whether or not his claim was approved. It is interesting to note that some of the bounty-land warrant claimants sold their rights to the land rather than move from a state to the public domain. The application records are divided into two principle series: the Revolutionary War series and the post-Revolutionary War series. Bounty-land benefits for veterans and their heirs after the Revolutionary War are based on numerous congressional acts. The last act approved on 3 March 1855 was by far the most liberal. If a veteran had served in a battle or for fourteen days he was eligible to receive 160 acres of land. The bounty-land warrant application files give such information as the soldier's name, rank, unit, period of service, age, residence, and occasionally, personal description. If the claim was filed by an heir, it also includes the name of the heir and the degree of relationship, and the place and date of the veteran's death. If the claim was approved, the file shows the warrant number, the number of acres granted, and the year of the corresponding congressional act.

THE PASSENGER ARRIVAL LISTS

One record source of particular interest to American families is the passenger lists of persons arriving from abroad at ports on the Atlantic Ocean or the Gulf of Mexico. These lists help identify the founders of families who arrived in America seeking the opportunity promised to all. Although there are lists for as early as 1798, most of them are for the years 1820-1945, but these contain many gaps. The San Francisco passenger lists were destroyed by fires in 1851 and 1940. The available lists consist of custom passenger lists, customs lists of aliens, and immigration passenger lists.

The federal government required ship captains to keep these early lists, and because of differences in bookkeeping methods between captains, the records vary considerably. Information on them also varies due to the laws under which the records were created and upon local custom. Usually a list will include the name of the ship, the name of the captain, the date and port of the ship's arrival, the name of the port of embarkation, and sometimes the date of embarkation. They also contain the name, age and occupation of each passenger.

While there are only a few passenger lists available before 1820, they are worth searching. Most of them concern arrivals from London, but some also note French, Spanish, and German emigration. During the colonial period in this country, persons from Germanic areas immigrated secretly through Dutch ports because of the laws restricting such travel. For this reason, records of many family founders are not recorded anywhere. In 1727 a law was enacted which required ship captains to make lists of alien passengers. It was at this time that many of the Germanic passengers were recorded.

After 1820 the passenger lists became voluminous. Almost all extant nineteenth century lists or microfilms thereof are located in the National Archives. These records are very difficult to search for several reasons. One is that the sheer mass of them prevents adequate investigation—for one year before the Civil War the lists recorded more than 300,000 arrivals. Another reason is that indexes have been destroyed or are incomplete or were never taken. An additional drawback to these records is that they do not include arrivals from Mexico, Canada, or persons who landed in the Great Lakes.

Because the indexes to the names on the passenger lists are incomplete and because many of the indexes to the immigration passenger lists are arranged chronologically, it is much easier to find the record of the arrival of a given person if the following information is known: the name of the port of entry, the name of the vessel, and the exact or approximate arrival date of the vessel. If the name of the port of entry and the approximate arrival date are known, it may be possible to determine the name of the vessel from the records or vessel entrances maintained at the ports and now in the National Archives. These volumes show the name of each vessel, the name of the captain, the name of the port of embarkation, and the date of the vessel's arrival. For some ports there are two series of volumes, in one of which the entries are arranged alphabetically by name of vessel and in the other, chronologically. In addition to the name of the port of entry and the approximate arrival date, if the port of embarkation is known, it is possible to narrow the search. For example, if a passenger embarked from Stockholm for New York in a year in which 500 passenger vessels arrived in New York, it would be possible to confine the search to the relatively few passenger lists for vessels sailing from Stockholm.

Naturalization records may aid in locating the passenger lists of immigrants who later petitioned for naturalization. Some naturalization records show for each petitioner his full name and the date and the name of the port of his arrival in the United States. The nineteenth century naturalization proceedings for the District of Columbia are in the National Archives. Records of naturalization proceedings in Federal courts outside of the District of Columbia are commonly to be found in records of the district court for the district in which the proceeding took place.

If the name of the court in which an immigrant was naturalized is not known, it may sometimes be learned from the lists of voters in the county where he resided. Whether such lists have been preserved may be determined for some counties through inventories of county records prepared by the Work Projects Administration. Inventories for some counties have been printed, and they are in the National Archives. Family records in private possession, such as journals or diaries, may also provide the information that will make an effective search possible.

MISCELLANEOUS RECORDS

In 1906 an order affecting United States embassies in foreign countries was given. This order required all consular posts to maintain records of registration for American citizens living abroad. The information contained in these records is the name of the citizen, the date and place of his birth, the identification of his wife, and the names and dates and places of birth of his children. Each record book has an index and these books are currently in the National Archives.

Another source of genealogical material is passport applications. Today these documents are made by an American citizen requesting the privilege of traveling outside the United States. But during the early years of this nation passports were issued to some persons wishing to travel from one state to another or from a state into Indian territory. These "passports" are generally testimonials as to the identification and the character of the bearer. They are very helpful to genealogists who claim pioneer ancestors who settled in the area that became Alabama, Mississippi, and Louisiana. Modern passport applications are received by the Department of State and then transferred to the National Archives. This practice began in 1791. They include the name of the applicant, his age, his date of birth, the place of his residence, and a personal description.

Land entry records, although they are of little genealogical value before 1862, may contain information about the migration of a family or individual. These records consist of documents which relate to rights or claims to land before grants or "patents" were issued by the federal government. A person could obtain title to a tract of land only after it was surveyed. After an individual obtained a certificate of title or its equivalent he was issued a patent. Copies of these patents are in the Bureau of Land Management in Washington, D.C.

It is easy to see why many people consider Washington, D.C. to be the "capital of genealogy." The city not only houses the documents of the nation, but it also contains most of the records of individuals. The serious researcher is encouraged to plan, if possible, to visit the city and study what is available to him in terms of "ancestor hunting." If a visit is not possible, requests by mail can be made by writing the addresses given in this chapter.

9

MISCELLANEOUS RECORDS . . .
CHURCHES, CEMETERIES, LODGES, ETC.

Ann I. Mahoney

Perhaps one of the most significant and fundamental aspects of research that a beginning genealogist quickly learns, and hopefully remembers, is simply that any source of information needs to be verified. In other words, just one source of data is not sufficient to state any fact "unequivocally." The more sources you have at hand to back up your findings, the more likely it is that your research will be accurate and valid. At times, locating additional, substantiating information is a difficult task, either because you're not sure how to use sources already available or you just don't know where to look for further data.

Within the scope of this chapter I plan to discuss a number of often unexplored genealogical reserves—including newspaper files, records of private organizations and societies, institutional and church records, and even cemetery gravestones—and to demonstrate how to most efficiently make use of these reserves. While these sources are frequently overlooked by the novice genealogist, they can often give you the necessary verification (or negation) of a fact, introduce a new clue that stimulates further research, or even provide that missing link.

Almost everyone reads a newspaper daily. Yet—partly because it's such an obvious store of genealogical wealth—it is frequently by-passed in the genealogist's research. And in many cases researchers prefer to consciously ignore this source of information because it can, in fact, be a tedious and difficult search. Fortunately, advancements made in microfilming are helping to make newspapers much more easily accessible to the researcher and, in addition, more and more newspapers are being indexed.

It is interesting to note that prior to 1689, there were no American newspapers. Up until that time all newspapers were imported from Europe. By 1763 there were twenty-three colonial newspapers, but not until that year did these newspapers really discuss the activities of the colonies. What kind of genealogical data can be provided by newspapers? Almost all newspapers devote columns to marriage and death notices. Additionally, a number of newspapers have special columns of queries and answers intended specifically for the genealogist. In 1876 the *Boston Evening Transcript* initiated a genealogical column that, by virtue of its popularity and usefulness, blossomed into an entire genealogical department in 1894, and was published for the next forty-seven years. Along with investigatory questions and answers, the *Transcript* also printed probate records, deed books, gravestone inscriptions, and entire genealogies. Much of this data has already been indexed and put on microfilm, ready and waiting for the industrious genealogist's probe.

Naturally, not all newspapers have as much to offer the genealogist as the *Transcript* and not all newspapers can be as easily searched. Nonetheless, a thriving interest in genealogy has made microfilming and indexing of newspapers more prevalent now than ever before. The American Antiquarian Society of Worcester, Massachusetts, is credited with being the first such organization to systematically probe genealogical data as revealed in newspapers. As pioneers in this field, perhaps their most outstanding achievement was the indexing of marriage and death notices in a Boston newspaper, the *Columbia Centinel*, for all issues published between 1784 and 1840. Most importantly, the *Centinel* published notices not just from the Boston area, but from all over the nation, so that the 80,000-name index has a very impressive national sampling of people. This index is currently available at two libraries—the New York Public Library and the Library of Congress—and at the New England Historic Genealogical

Society. Other early newspapers also indexed by the American Antiquarian Society include the *New York Weekly Museum* (1788-1817), the *Christian Intelligencer* (1830-1871), and the *Boston Evening Transcript* (1879-1899).

Since the initial steps taken by the American Antiquarian Society, a number of individuals and organizations have made progress toward shaping American newspaper files into both a genealogical tool and a genealogical source. Available at the Library of Congress are several newspaper indexes compiled and published by the Works Progress Administration, including one of the *Virginia Gazette* (1735-1780) and a twenty-seven volume index to newspapers printed in Savannah, Georgia, during the years 1763 and 1830. Also available at the Library of Congress are two "check lists" of American newspapers, both printed by the Genealogical Publishing Company.

Newspaper indexes covering a broader spectrum are, by their very nature, in greater demand and, consequently, available at a far greater number of libraries. Ayer's *Newspaper Guide,* Gregory's *Union List of American Newspapers 1821-1936,* and Brigham's *History and Bibliography of American Newspaper 1690-1820,* to name but a few, can be found in most public libraries. An excellent aid in discovering what newspapers are on microfilm is Richard W. Hale's *Guide to Photocopied Historical Materials in the United States and Canada,* published by Cornell University Press in 1961.

Hunting for facts in newspapers is not always easy, but often rewarding. The prime disadvantage of newspaper research—lack of indexes—is now being earnestly tackled, so that in the near future this storehouse of genealogical data will be just as useful as any other indexed volume. But in addition to searching for marriage the death records in newspapers, newspapers can also serve as a medium through which a genealogist can present his queries to literally thousands of people at a time. Advertising your investigation in a newspaper (particularly in a genealogical publication) is one of the most expedient modes of research available to the genealogist.

If, for instance, you need a piece of information on your

great-grandfather, but you've already exhausted all local records and still need to fill in some blank spaces, possibly your next profitable step would be to advertise for facts about your great-grandfather in the local paper of the town nearest to where he lived. The responses to your query could provide those missing links, and even if nothing comes from it, the amount of time and money you've spent would have been minimal. As mentioned in another chapter, don't forget to check for newspapers published by family organizations and associations; these obviously, are directed specifically to genealogical inquiries and answers, and the exchange of information made possible by these newspapers is phenomenal. Newspapers are intended to relay facts to a mass audience and only need your active participation to make them serviceable to your needs.

Another source of data also available to the public, but often left only to collect dust, are the records of private organizations, clubs, and societies. The amount and type of data these records provide differ to a degree, but because of the very nature of their membership requirements, they can be most informative to the genealogist. The Masons, Elks, Odd Fellows, and Knights of Columbus are all fraternal organizations which have records dating back to their inception. Additionally, the Kiwanis, Rotary, and Lions clubs provide similar, although not as complete, records. The kind of genealogical information compiled in their files may be as simple as the member's name and date and place of joining. However, many of these records also include the names of the member's parents, wife, and children (and even sometimes with their birthdates), and detailed biographical descriptions that include the member's educational background, occupation, and religious affiliation. Some of these membership records also include photographs.

Here is one source of information that, at the least, can confirm the whereabouts of your subject at a given time and, at the best, can not only provide numerous essential facts, but also fill out your subject's personality, making the study of genealogy more than just an exercise in dates and numbers—rather, making it an exciting study of human nature. All the genealogist has to do to explore these records is contact the local secretary of any particular organization; if the secretary does not have the files you're seeking at hand, he undoubtedly can direct you to the proper sources.

College fraternities also keep excellent membership files, particularly because fraternities usually give priority consideration for membership to the children of their current members. Kappa Alpha Society is the oldest social fraternity in America, introduced at Union College (New York) in 1825. Phi Beta Kappa, an academic fraternity, has records dating as far back as 1776. Like the fraternal societies and organizations mentioned above, these college fraternities keep records that contain much genealogical data, with, obviously, an emphasis on a member's educational background. To gain access to these files a genealogist need only contact the secretary of a local chapter of the fraternity or correspond with the National Interfraternity Conference. In addition, Baird's *Manual of American College Fraternities* (available at almost all public libraries) is an invaluable tool for determining which fraternities are currently active or inactive and, on a yearly basis, which fraternities are at which colleges. This information can be a real timesaver. University clubs, which require their members to have a college degree, also keep extensive files on the educational background of their members.

Frequently old estate records show expenditures made for schooling and many early school records are still intact, including those of some of the very oldest schools in the country—Roxbury Latin School (Roxbury, Massachusetts), William Penn Charter School (Philadelphia, Pennsylvania), and Boston Latin School (Boston, Massachusetts). Harvard University, William and Mary College, and Yale University—three of the oldest colleges in America—have rosters, rolls, yearbooks, and enrollment records dating back to their founding. These files usually show the student's residence and give the names of his parents or guardians.

To locate educational files the genealogist can start at his own public library by checking out a number of extensive school directories, including Marsh's *American Colleges and Universities,* Good's *Guide to Colleges, Universities, and Pro-*

fessional Schools in the United States, and Patterson's *American Education Dictionary.* For another approach, once you've determined your subject's residence, simply check local records to determine what schools were operating at that time. Prior to the establishment of a public school system, many schools were religiously affiliated. To narrow down the field of choices, start with the school of your subject's religious background. Files for records of institutions now inactive or extinct can usually be found at the church that supported the school, at the state historical society or archives, or at the National Archives.

School records are at times limited in their scope, but nonetheless, they can provide the necessary verification that a genealogist is constantly in search of. Occasionally they provide extensive biographical details. In addition, numerous directories have been compiled on private and public institutions (the date and locale of their founding and the years of their existence) and are of a great aid to genealogists. Directories, while in and of themselves are dry and boring lists of facts, should be consulted whenever possible; they can prove to be as useful as road maps are to a lost motorist. City, telephone, professional, and trade directories are all capable of pointing you in the right direction. To get an idea of the extensive scope of city directories alone, just check Dorothea Spear's *Bibliography of American Directories Through 1860.* Published compilations of this nature make the genealogist's task so much less of a "wild goose chase," so whenever possible, take advantage of research already done for you. Delve with enthusiasm into any records—those of hospitals, associations, business and professional organizations, etc.—that appear relevant to your own personal inquiry. To the extreme benefit of the genealogist, more and more organizations are keeping detailed records of their members. Some of the newer organizations (in particular, professional societies and societies exclusively for women) may not have records at this point which are old enough to be of value to today's genealogist, but they will unquestionably prove to be a new and valuable source for future generations.

Church records are as old as the churches themselves and

church directories have been published by virtually every denomination. The history of church records is a fascinating one, directly related to the history of surname formation, another field of interest for the genealogist. The keeping of fastidious church records is an American custom borrowed from the Europeans. For centuries members of religious orders—monks and priests—were an elite group of men by virtue of their reading and writing skills. In England in the late 1200s, for example, clerks were hired to keep land and church registers of every parish so that the monarchs of the nation could levy taxes. As a result, church clerks began to compile written records of surnames, writing these names in their natural, rather than Latin, form. This process of documentation had the effect of causing a great flux in the adoption of surnames, as well as the effect of stabilizing surnames. Early records of this nature which are still in existence today and many of which have been published, date as far back as 1273. They not only show a clear pattern of how and to what degree certain surnames were adopted, but also provide a priceless bank of genealogical data—birth and death dates, land ownership, deeds and wills, etc. Parliament passed an act in 1538 which literally required clerks of the church to record all christenings, marriages, and burials.

Fortunately for historians and genealogists, this custom of recording parish activities has been continued in America from the formation of the colonies up through present times. While for the most part these records are considered highly accurate and reliable, gaps are frequent because many church records have been lost or accidentally destroyed and some are simply illegible (another reason why the serious genealogist should make the effort to have all of his findings typewritten and duplicated whenever possible). Other church records are incomplete, especially in cases where a parish had only a temporary or circuit pastorate; often when a traveling minister left a parish or was relocated to another parish, he would take all the records with him and forget to return them to that parish.

A degree of inaccuracy or error was introduced if a minister was not present at the time of some event; he would record the event only after his return to the congregation and only from secondhand knowledge. Thus it is easy to understand how these records could fail to register an event or register it incorrectly. On the other hand, many of these records are highly esteemed for their degree of validity because they were recorded as the event occurred.

Again, the amount of information provided by church records varies greatly from one denomination to another. Most records provide baptismal dates of a subject, but along with this, many also give the subject's birthdate and place, and the name of one or both of the subject's parents (or the name of a witness, sponsor, or guardian). It should be remembered, however, that if one parent was not a member of the church, that parent's name would not likely appear in the records. If you were searching through baptismal records to find out how many children a couple had, you must remember that all of their children would not necessarily be recorded if the couple joined a particular parish after some of their children had already been baptized. This is an excellent opportunity to warn the genealogist never to take any one source of information as the "ultimate truth." While the source may be valid, authentic, and reliable, by itself it can also be misleading.

Church records almost always register marriages (which usually give the parents' names [especially when the couples being married are young] and the names of witnesses), but even more consistently, they register the posting of marriage banns. Here again there is room for error if not recorded properly by the genealogist—it must be remembered that an intention to marry is not the same thing as a marriage, and this distinction should be noted. The third most frequently recorded event in church registers is burial dates, along with which frequently appears the death date (another fine distinction that needs to be noted to avoid confusion).

If membership lists are included, as they usually are, records of confirmations or admissions to the parish are also available. These records can also include your subject's prior affiliation or residence and in the case of transference, your subject's destination to another parish. Many churches diligently record all proceedings and activities within the church, including church officers and delegates, and disciplinary measures. Some parish registers also have a list of charity donations.

The scope of these early records is particularly impressive when viewed in an historical context. In early America a greater majority of citizens were actively involved with the affairs of their parish, if for no other reason than the fact that the church—as one of the few institutions available to the colonists—was often the real center of community life; in turn, churches were particularly active in the affairs of local governments. Hopefully it is clear just how abundant in genealogical data church records can be. The next step, of course, is locating those records. For a general overview of the situation, there are several outstanding church directories which can be consulted, including E. Kay Kirkham's *A Survey of American Church Records;* also available (at the Library of Congress) is a compilation of church records from various denominations and in various states published by the Works Progress Administration. And, as stated earlier, many denominations published their own directories.

For records of churches which are still in operation, first contact the pastor of that church. While he may not have the records on hand, he undoubtedly will be able to direct you to their location. These records are generally stored by an active church organization or by a local historical society; infrequently they are held by private individuals who are closely associated with the church (i.e., a parish clerk). For records of churches which are no longer in operation, first contact the nearest historical society. If you are unsuccessful there, check to see if the particular denomination maintains archives for now defunct churches; most church bodies do. Your final check would be to a state organization of the church—a central governing agency. In the case of very old church records, frequently local libraries or municipal agencies store the files.

The following brief discussion is intended to provide a sampling of where and what kinds of church records are maintained by various denominations. The early Puritans kept baptismal and burial records, but no marriage records.

This reveals an interesting bit of history: marriage to the Puritans was not conceived as a religious sacrament, but rather as a civil contract, and at one point ministers were literally forbidden to perform the marriage ceremony. The church did, however, post banns of marriage.

The Quakers are noted for their detailed accounts of church activities and in their registers are extensive records of birth, marriages, deaths, and transfer (an excellent clue to trace a subject's former residence or migration to a new area). The *Encyclopedia of American Quaker Genealogy* is an excellent genealogical tool, as is the Friends Historical Association founded at Swarthmore College in Pennsylvania. The Methodist church houses much of its genealogical data at Drew Theological Seminary in Madison, New Jersey, while the Episcopal church prefers to keep its records at the local parish or diocese. The American Jewish Archives are quite extensive, as is the Jewish Central Library in London, England. The Baptist church maintains most of its records at Colgate University in Hamilton, New York, and in Philadelphia, Pennsylvania, at the American Baptist Historical Library. Presbyterian registers are filed by the Presbyterian Historical Society in Philadelphia, and the Lutheran church, noted for its extensive records of marriages and genealogical data on the children of its members, stores most of its records at the Society of the United Lutheran Church in America, located in Gettysburg, Pennsylvania. In 1935 Cora C. Curry published a useful guide to records of the Roman Catholic Church entitled *Records of the Roman Catholic Church in the United States As a Source for Authentic Genealogical and Historical Material.*

Perhaps the most extensive church records of a genealogical nature are those kept by the Church of Jesus Christ of the Latter-day Saints, whose center is in Salt Lake City. The reason for their thoroughness is in part explained by the dogmas of the faith: as part of their creed Mormons are required to keep a complete and accurate record of their immediate family and to trace their direct line of ancestry as far back as possible. In 1894 several members of the church organized a genealogical society to aid in carrying out this legacy and by

1944 it was incorporated under the name of the Genealogical Society of the Church of Jesus Christ of the Latter-day Saints. While under the direct auspices of the church, its resources are open to the general public. Within its library the Mormon church keeps records of births, marriages, and deaths from family Bibles, diaries, hymnals, and other sources. As early as 1938 the Mormons began the demanding task of putting all of this data—collected not only from the United States, but from across the world—on microfilm. By 1960 this collection encompassed 246,838, 100-foot rolls of film and the library already had 150 microfilm readers. The project is to be continued indefinitely and the magnitude of its scope and its worth to the genealogist is truly overwhelming. Not all church documents are as thorough and easy to use as those just described, but almost every denomination does have records from which essential genealogical data can be obtained.

The topics so far discussed in this chapter have all dealt with the exploration of written records which are frequently overlooked by the novice researcher. The final topic of this chapter—gravestones as a source of genealogical data—is of a slightly different nature. Here we are dealing with what a researcher calls primary, original, or raw material. For the time being we can forget about libraries, records, and files, and take a trip outdoors to do research. Cemeteries are, in fact, storehouses of genealogical and historical information and for generations have created a genealogical pastime. They are particularly valuable sources of information when municipal death records or church burial records have been destroyed.

While some people may hesitate at the thought of visiting a graveyard, its value to genealogists cannot be ignored and it certainly need not be an unpleasant experience. Graves are marked so that an individual, in his death, can be remembered by the living; a visit to a cemetery can activate this remembrance. It is interesting to note that several cities across the nation are planning to make several large cemeteries into park areas, not in disrespect to the dead, but in mutual respect for the deceased, for the land, and for the living.

Many old, private cemeteries have been neglected because families of the deceased have moved to other parts of the country. But in early America, when people were less mobile and one family lived in the same locale for several generations, whole families were buried together, often on their own land. This fact is particularly valuable to the genealogist who, in searching for records of one particular ancestor, may discover the gravestones of other, related individuals. The first step in approaching this type of research is to determine the approximate death date and place of your subject. Most local historical societies will then be able to tell you which cemeteries were in use at that time. Note should be taken to check cemeteries of neighboring towns as well, since the boundary lines have probably altered somewhat from the original survey lines. You might eliminate some choices by starting with a cemetery affiliated with the religious denomination of your subject.

When you visit a cemetery, come equipped to tackle the weathering effects of time on a gravestone. In other words, stones may need to be cleared of moss and underbrush before they can be read. If you plan to photograph a headstone, bring chalk to trace over the lettering so that it will show up clearly in your picture. If you wish to make a rubbing of the stone, for the best results bring wrapping paper and either a marking crayon or a soft lead pencil.

Headstones can be difficult to read, usually because of the effects of age or because of the style in which the inscriptions were made. If read incorrectly, confusion will abound, so a special effort should be made to be as accurate as possible. Always copy the stone exactly as it is written—letter for letter, word for word—including all punctuation. These precautions should be taken to narrow or eliminate the margin for error. If parts of the inscription are illegible, indicate this on your transcript.

Gravestones of the late 1700s were hand chiseled in roman letter on a dark slate. While this lettering was easy to read, the stones were easily split and weathered. In the early 1800s a harder, grayish-blue slate was used, but the change to a very difficult to read italic script has rendered many of these stones illegible. In the 1840s hard marble was used and in the later 1800s granite was employed. More recent gravestones have sandblast inscriptions, which survive the longest by far.

The basic information provided on a gravestone—death date and approximate age—has been consistently retained through the years, but stated or worded differently, so that it can at times lead to confusion. The age statement is not always exact: "died aged seventeen years" does not mean precisely the same thing as "died in her seventeenth year." If you are not given or cannot figure out the exact age of your subject, it is almost always possible to approximate that age. Occasionally you may discover a stone that gives not only the year, month, and day of your subject's death, but also the hour. In the case of a child, the gravestone usually mentions the names of the child's parents (and the child's grave is usually situated close of his parents' graves). In the case of a married woman, her husband's name is generally given.

In studying headstones, always view them in association with surrounding gravestones and never assume too much from one marker; chances for error enter if the stone is difficult to read and if the original marker has at one time been replaced by a newer one. In addition, because of the expense involved in having a stone inscribed and erected, occasionally blatant errors in the inscription are left unaltered. You should also search the sexton's records. These files often indicate who purchased the lot, who pays for its upkeep, and who currently owns the lot. These files also have a complete record of all burials in the cemetery and the location of all graves. Records of now defunct cemeteries are usually held by a local historical society.

While the typical gravestone reveals few personal characteristics of your subject beyond his age, the date of his death, and possibly the name of a relative, frequently you will find short or even lengthy inscriptions which provide a clue to his personality. A visit to a cemetery can help you to verify facts you already have, or present new ones. And in judging the simplicity or the splendor of the stone, you often gain an insight into the lives of an entire family.

Whether you're searching for facts in cemeteries, in libraries, in books, or in some long forgotten files, the genealogical quest can be exciting and rewarding. Just two points need to be reemphasized. Nine times out of ten, the sources are available, it's just a matter of taking the ingenuity to discover where these genealogical reserves can be found and taking the time to learn how to use them expediently. Hopefully this chapter has clarified the use of sources you were uncertain about or has revealed possible new material. Hopefully, too, you've been encouraged to think of even more avenues to probe. This most successful genealogists are undoubtedly those who are able to keep an open mind in seeking all available channels of research. Secondly, never rely on just one source of information. This in itself should help stimulate a constant search for new sources of data. One source, by itself, is insufficient simply because records are frequently erroneous, incomplete, or misleading. The good genealogist must always strive for validity and accuracy, and knowing how to find and utilize all available records makes his task both challenging and rewarding.

10

HERALDRY

J. Charles Thompson

The connection between heraldry and genealogy is closer than most people realize. The difference between heraldic devices and those used earlier on armor and elsewhere is genealogical. True heraldry began only when a man would use the same device throughout his lifetime and pass it on to his heir. The herald considers furthermore that genealogy is part of heraldry. The study of coats of arms—which most people consider to be heraldry—is only part of the herald's specialty, and he calls that part "armory." To satisfy a pedantic herald, the title of this chapter should have been "Armory," because coats of arms are what we will be discussing. We are not writing for pedantic heralds, however, but for people who will be better pleased with the title of "Heraldry," which we have used.

The first warning the heraldist must give the genealogist is: don't try to trace your "family coats of arms!" There is no such thing as family arms, at least in British heraldry. Each man's arms are his own and are passed on to his heir, usually his oldest son. The younger sons (cadets) will change the arms in some way, and these differenced arms will be passed on to the eldest son of each of them. Younger sons of each generation will add further differences to the arms, so that no two men's arms will be just alike.

If your line traces back to a nobleman, or to a Sir John "somebody," he will of course have borne arms. (To keep things brief, we need the word "armiger"—a person who has used a coat of arms.) Armigers, except noblemen and knights, will be identified by the title of Gentleman, abbreviated Gent., or Esquire (Esq.). If you find a legal document mentioning, for example, James Babcock, Gent. and Thomas Suffolk, you can be sure that James Babcock was an armigerous gentleman, and Thomas Suffolk was not, in spite of his distinguished surname.

This distinction has disappeared over the last couple of centuries. The title of Gentleman is almost never used today, and the use of Esquire has spread. Foreign service officers of the Department of State and the mayors of some cities are properly known as John Doe, Esq., and these are just two examples. Yet most such esquires have never been armigerous. In addition to the correct use of the title, almost any company or society in Britain will address its customers or members as Esquire, and the same title is often used in the United States to give a pseudo-British flavor to correspondence.

What does it mean, though, if you find an armiger among your ancestors? The arms of this gentleman are not your arms unless you are his heraldic heir, that is unless you are the eldest son of the eldest son, all the way back to the original armiger. Of course, if the eldest son died without children, the arms would pass to his next brother, but unless you are the senior male descendant, they are not your arms. If you have the same surname as the ancestral armiger, you are entitled to a differenced version of the arms. If you can prove this direct male descent, you may want to get in touch with the College of Arms in London, or the Lord Lyon in Edinburgh. Upon proper proof of descent from an armigerous Englishman or Scot, the appropriate authority will grant you a coat of arms based on the original.

That procedure is not often available, because the vast majority of the immigrants to America were not gentlemen (in the strictly armorial sense of the word). If you are the descendant of a grantee of arms, the appropriate authority (the College of Arms or the Lord Lyon) thereby has jurisdiction to consider your case. However, they will grant new arms if you can prove descent to anyone, armigerous or not, who came under their jurisdiction: this means a male ancestor in the direct line, with the same surname you now bear. But the proof of descent must be documented, as must the description of each male ancestor. If you claim descent from or through Doctor Doe or Colonel Roe, you will be expected to present proof of his degree or commission. There are stiff fees for the grant of arms, and preparation of the proofs will add to them. If you have a few hundred dollars to spare—maybe even a thousand or more—this is the way to get a grant of arms that no one can possibly question. In addition, you will get a parchment certificate with some of the best heraldic art being produced these days.

If you want arms and cannot afford these prices, there is still another way. It is not commonly known, and we will discuss the reasons in detail later in this chapter, but any American who wants arms of his own can properly design his own and start using them. That is not quite as simple as it sounds, because of two things. Firstly, you must be positive that the arms have not been used by anyone else before you. Otherwise you would be usurping his arms, which is always wrong. In Scotland usurping arms will land you in the Lyon Court, faced with a stiff fine. Secondly, if you try to design your own arms, get the advice of a competent heraldist. Proper design of new arms is a complex art, and anyone trying it without long study is likely to end with arms that will be an object of derision to the better informed.

Unfortunately, the current interest in heraldry in the United States has given rise to many abuses. Many Americans have the mistaken impression that, because a particular coat of arms was borne by someone who had the same surname as themselves, they are entitled to use those arms. There is some basis for this in Irish practice. The Herald of Ireland says that you may use the arms of the chief of your name if you can show that you are descended from him or one of his ancestors. But with English and Scottish arms, the case is entirely different. In the first place, as the AGRI publications point out, there are several, sometimes dozens of coats of arms for every common surname, each the property of a different individual or branch of the family. There is absolutely nothing wrong with displaying the arms of someone of your surname, but you may not say that those are your *personal* arms. But we will cover this in more detail later on.

Some organizations in this country offer to grant you arms. In this case the arms *will* be individual and often well designed. But the price will probably be exorbitant—several hundred dollars. The catch here is that nobody except a sovereign or a sovereign state can properly authorize anyone to grant arms. The United States Congress has never given any such authorization, nor as far as I can determine, has any state in the Union. But when the company is described as "incorporated under the laws of the State of . . . for the purpose of granting arms," the implication is that the arms are in some way official. This implication is entirely false, but it is the only grounds for charges that are in the same range as those levied by the College of Arms in London, or the Lord Lyon in Edinburgh.

This does not mean you should never get help by mail in designing your own arms. Just be sure of two things: that the arms are truly individual and that the design is good heraldry. An example of bad heraldry is a shield divided in quarters with a different device in each quarter. As we will see later, a shield should be quartered only when combining the arms of two families or institutions. Quartering the shield of one individual shows a complete lack of understanding of the principles of heraldic design.

When you have avoided all the pitfalls and finally arrived at well-designed and distinctive arms for yourself, how can you protect them from infringement? Unfortunately, you cannot. You can copyright one drawing of your arms, but (again as we will see later) the same arms can be drawn in very different ways, depending on the style and skill of the artist. Another representation of the arms will not infringe the copyright. This seems unfair until we examine a parallel. If I take and copyright a photograph of the president of the United States, this does not prevent someone else from taking and publishing another picture of the president. Just as two photographs of the same man cannot be illegal under copyright laws, so two drawings of the same arms do not conflict.

How about registration as a trademark? Firstly, before you can register your arms as a trademark, they must have been used to mark goods in interstate commerce. That is not what they were designed for, but even if you used them so, registration as a trademark would only prevent someone else from using them to mark goods in commerce. If you wanted to copy the trademark of Pall Mall cigarettes (which are arms of a sort) and hang them on your wall as your own arms, it might be humorous, but it would be in no way illegal.

Any arms you design and use will become part of a long and honorable tradition. Decorated shields go back at least to the ancient Greeks. The Tudor and Jacobean heralds let their enthusiasm go as far as describing the arms of the Biblical ancients back to Adam and Eve. But none of this was true heraldry. At least down to the Norman William the Bastard, who became the English William the Conqueror, a man might change his device each time he got a new shield. The reason was simple: even in full battle gear you could see his face. When the rumor flew at the Battle of Hastings that William had been killed, he simply lifted his helmet by the nose-piece, and everybody could see that he was still there, alive and fighting. Imagine what would have happened if he had been wearing a closed helmet, laced and riveted to his body armor!

It was this closed helmet that raised the problem of quick battlefield identification, and the problem was solved by heraldry. Each knight adopted a device and wore it on a coat that covered his armor (his coat of arms) and painted it on his shield. He did not change it between battles, because that would have defeated its very purpose. He also pictured it (examples date back to 1138) on the seal he used, because he couldn't sign his name, and a seal was both more elegant and more foolproof than a mark X. When his heir inherited the estate, he would continue to use the same seal and would also use his father's arms in battle. Random devices thus developed into true heraldry: arms that a man maintained throughout his lifetime and passed on to his heir.

One important feature of early heraldry is often passed

over in the usual histories. The knights adopted their own arms, without regard to heralds or anyone else. The heralds got into the act because they were in charge of tournaments and other ceremonies where the knights turned out in full battle array. The heralds had to announce each knight as he appeared, so they were forced to learn and keep in mind the devices that each knight wore. The knights naturally tried to keep their arms different from anyone else's, because the prime purpose of the arms was to keep them separate from each other. But duplications were bound to occur.

The most notorious of these was the Scrope vs. Grosvenor case, and we will describe it briefly here, for two reasons. It illustrates some very important points, and writers also keep quoting it, assuming that the reader knows the facts of the case. Briefly, when the English knights gathered in the time of Richard II for the foreign wars, two of them were using the same device: a gold stripe diagonally across a blue shield (azure, a bend or). Their contest over the right to these arms occupied the Court of Chivalry for five years, 1385-1390. Finally the court awarded the arms to Scrope and told Grosvenor he could use the same arms, but with a silver border. Grosvenor refused and appealed to King Richard II, who confirmed the decision of the court. Now comes the interesting part: instead of accepting the arms granted by the court and confirmed by the king, Grosvenor took new arms on his own authority: a golden sheaf of wheat on blue (azure, a garb or). The point to note is that the authorities could tell Grosvenor what arms he must not use, but could not dictate the arms he should use.

Central control over arms was gradually established. In 1418 a writ of Henry V forbade anyone to "assume . . . coats of arms, unless . . . in right of his ancestors, or by the gift of some person having adequate power." So after nearly three centuries of each man assuming and using the arms he chose, the Crown took over the function of granting arms. Late in the same century, Richard III incorporated the heralds into a College of Arms, which functions to this day. These were and are persons "having adequate power" to grant arms, and no one questions the validity of a grant from the College. However, there was no law passed making other arms illegal, and some authorities still contend that assuming arms in England today is not only perfectly legal, but perfectly proper.

The same is not true in Scotland. In 1672 the Scottish Parliament established the Lord Lyon, whose office had existed for three centuries, as the sole authority to grant arms in Scotland. Anyone in Scotland usurping another man's arms or designing bogus arms for himself can be haled into the Lyon Court and fined. If he persists in defying the power of the court, he can also be imprisoned.

As time went on, coats of arms lost their function of identification in battle. As firearms came in, closed helmets went out. Tournaments became mere shows, and arms no longer served as an instant means of identification. This had two results. Coats of arms became more detailed and complex, to the point that they were decorative rather than distinctive. Secondly, the need for a man to be distinguished from his brothers became less of a consideration.

In the old days, brothers could turn up on different sides of the same battle, and the younger had to have a difference in his arms as a matter of sheer survival. In Scotland, arms of cadets are still differenced, and the system used permits the expert to examine the arms of two men of the same family and determine just how they are related to each other. In England, on the other hand, differencing by cadets has become entirely optional. Some men prize their individuality, but others feel that it is enough if their arms are those of their own branch of the family.

Another change was the result of arms becoming mostly drawings. The crest that is drawn above the shield started as a device that the knight actually wore on the top of his helmet. This would rise above the confusion of battle, even if his shield was not visible. Early crests were usually some device that could have been modelled in leather or light wood and attached to the helmet. Other possible crests were feathers, or some device painted on either side of a flat metal crest running along the ridge of the helm. But when coats of arms were only drawings or architectural carvings, crests could be almost anything. One example was a hand descending from the clouds holding a laurel wreath as the reward of valor.

Another example of poor heraldry of this period was the use of names or other writing. Heraldry started as instant identification for—we must admit—illiterates. So the name of a battle on the shield of the victor is perhaps even worse than the picture of the Battle of the Nile that appears at the top of Lord Nelson's shield.

The Romantic Revival in Queen Victoria's time brought on a renewed interest in heraldry. It also saw the revival of heraldic scholarship and a tendency to reform the worst practices of the preceding years. The biggest controversy of this period was over assumed arms. We have seen that knights assumed their own arms for the first three centuries of heraldic history. Arms could be granted, but this was a special favor. If the King or some high noble told a knight what arms he could use, this was esteemed as an honor. Most of the time, that is; we have seen that Grosvenor rejected arms that Richard II had approved for him, but that was surely exceptional. However, Grosvenor did what knights had been doing for centuries—took arms that he liked, and as long as they did not conflict with someone else's everybody was happy with them.

Once the College of Arms was formed, they tried to establish control of arms that were being used. Heralds went out on "visitations" to record arms. It is not quite clear what the requirements were before they consented to record the arms. Apparently if your grandfather had used the arms, the heralds would put them down. There was no definite test. If a farmer was using new arms, he would probably be told to stop, but the heralds do not seem to have been as strict with a bigger landowner. In any case, if the arms were well established, the heralds never said, "You have to stop using them because nobody ever granted them to anybody." And there seem to have been cases when a visiting herald told people to stop using arms, and they kept right on using them anyway.

Yet some Victorian authorities, several centuries later,

took the position that no arms that had not been properly granted by a sovereign or his duly appointed herald were genuine arms. The situation differs, of course, with the location. In Scotland, the right to grant arms was vested in the Lord Lyon in 1672. Any arms assumed in Scotland are definitely illegal; "bogus" is the technical word. If you can prove, however, that you are using arms that were used in Scotland before 1672 and that you are the heir of the original user, they are your arms without question.

The word "bogus" is interesting. Its commonest use is in coinage, and it does not mean the same thing as "counterfeit." If you started minting dimes just like the dimes currently produced by the United States government, these would be counterfeit dimes. But if you started producing dimes with President Truman's head on one side and your own design on the back, these would be "bogus" dimes. They would look like genuine American coins without exactly imitating any genuine issue.

The parallel with arms is exact. Using someone else's arms, exactly as he assumed them or had them granted is the same thing as counterfeiting a coin. In the language of armory, this is called "usurping" his arms. This is never right, proper, or correct in any country under any circumstances, unless you are also claiming ownership to the man's land and other property. You have no more business using another man's arms than you would have using his toothbrush—they are his property and just as truly personal property.

Using arms you have designed yourself is parallel with bogus coinage. They resemble genuine arms without exactly duplicating any arms that have been granted. There is only one catch. Where there is no genuine item, there can be no bogus. In Scotland, where the law provides that only arms granted by the Lord Lyon are genuine, any other arms are bogus by definition. Even in Scotland, however, a person who has assumed arms in the United States or elsewhere may use them freely, with two provisos. They must not be anybody else's genuine arms, since this would be usurping arms which is contrary to Scottish law. Secondly, the user must not be a national or resident of Scotland. This would bring him under the jurisdiction of the Lyon Court, and he would have to petition for the grant of the arms. The Lord Lyon will not comment on what arms might be granted until a petition has been made, but he would be likely to grant the arms as they have been used unless there is some reason not to.

The position of bogus arms in England is less clear. The College of Arms is undoubtedly authorised to grant arms, but there is clearly no law against using other arms. Even usurping arms is not punishable under English law. Some take the position, therefore, that there is no such thing as bogus arms in England. The College of Arms emphatically disagrees. If you have been using arms and approach them for a grant, they will insist on some change in the arms. There must be some slight addition, or a change in some color. Otherwise, the College would consider that they had legitimated bogus arms, which they refuse to do. This is a ticklish question, which no expert can settle. The position of the College of Arms is unequivocal, but it is not backed by law. If you absolutely refuse to let them make any change in the arms you are using, you are in somewhat the same position as Grosvenor was. They will not grant you the arms you want, but they cannot prevent you in any way from continuing to use them.

In the United States, the position is as clear as it is in Scotland, but very different. There is clearly no authority to grant arms, so the question of bogus arms does not arise. We are absolutely in the same position as the early knights. No one can grant arms, so we can use what we will. There is no genuine "coinage" so there can be no bogus. There is no law, either, to prevent us from usurping another person's arms. The only deterrent is the opinion and regard of people who know something about the subject. If you hang the Duke of Norfolk's arms on your wall and say, "They're mine, because my name is Howard," you will appear pretty uninformed to anyone who knows much about heraldry. Remember, though, if you display the same arms and say, "They belong to the principal family of the name of Howard, and I like them because I am a Howard, too," you are acting perfectly reasonably and sensibly.

Since Victorian times, the interest in arms has continued, and nowhere more than in the United States today. If you really want to learn about armory, there are many excellent books and articles, a few of them listed at the end of this chapter. But any genealogist should know a little about the subject, and the brief sketch that follows is at least a good start.

The proper term for the complete arms including everything that appears in the drawing with them is "achievement." Few except heraldists use the word in this sense, and it is not wrong to say "coat of arms." The heraldist would rather say that the design on the shield is the "coat of arms," since that is what the knight would have had on the coat he wore over his armor, but almost everyone uses "coat of arms" and "achievement" interchangeably. It is not correct, however, to call the achievement a crest. The crest is only part of the achievement, what the knight used to wear on top of his helmet. So calling any achievement a "family crest" will mark you as someone who knows little about heraldry.

The basis of all arms is the shield, or "escutcheon." It carries the device that marks the man, and no arms are complete without the shield. It can carry many different devices, called "charges," some of which are discussed below.

The next most important element of the achievement is the crest. This was formerly worn on the top of the helmet, and the heraldist likes to see a crest that could have been worn that way. It is quite common, particularly in the early crests, to see only the head or top half of an animal or bird. To fit the bottom of a pointed shield, a lion might balance on one foot with three in the air, or an eagle might have a spindly tail coming down past his feet. For the top of the helm, however, this would be a bit precarious, and the neck or waist covering the whole top of the helmet gave a much more sure support. You can have a shield without a crest, but a crest has no separate existence apart from the shield. The crest may be used separately on stationery or jewelry, but if you say, "I have a crest of my own, but there is no shield that goes with it," you are making it pretty clear that you don't know much heraldry. When shown separately, the crest should always rest on the wreath or crown that surrounded its base on a real helmet. The English used to insist that younger sons difference the crest as well as the arms, but in Scottish practice the cadets often use the same crest and motto as the heir.

The third main element of an achievement is the motto. In English heraldry it is usually shown under the shield, but the Scots prefer a scroll around the helmet and crest. There may be more than one motto, in which case one will be shown below and one above. The motto is not fixed and constant. A man may adopt a new motto whenever he will. The motto may be in any language. English, French, and Latin are the commonest, but Gaelic mottoes abound in Scotland, and mottoes in Greek, and even languages as remote as Hindustani are not unknown. The meaning of the motto is often unclear. One crest shows a man's head impaled on a sword, and the motto is "Think on." Cunningham's motto, "Over, fork over," has never been well explained. The common story is that the man who took the motto once escaped his enemies by being buried in the hay, but there is no historical record that this ever happened, and it is more common for a motto to refer to a more glorious happening or sentiment. "Virture mine honor" or "Victory or death" are more typical mottoes.

Between the shield and crest you will usually see a helm and mantling. "Helm" and "helmet" mean the same thing, and you will sometimes see the French word *lambrequin* used instead of "mantling." The old knights needed to wear a cloth over their helmets when they went out in the sun, and this was the mantling. It was held on by a crown, or a twist of cloth known as the "torse" or wreath. In British heraldry the form of the helmet tells you something about a man's rank: monarch, peer, knight, or gentleman. None of these apply in America, so the form of the helmet and the mantling as well is left up to the individual artist. As a matter of fact, many Americans like to display their

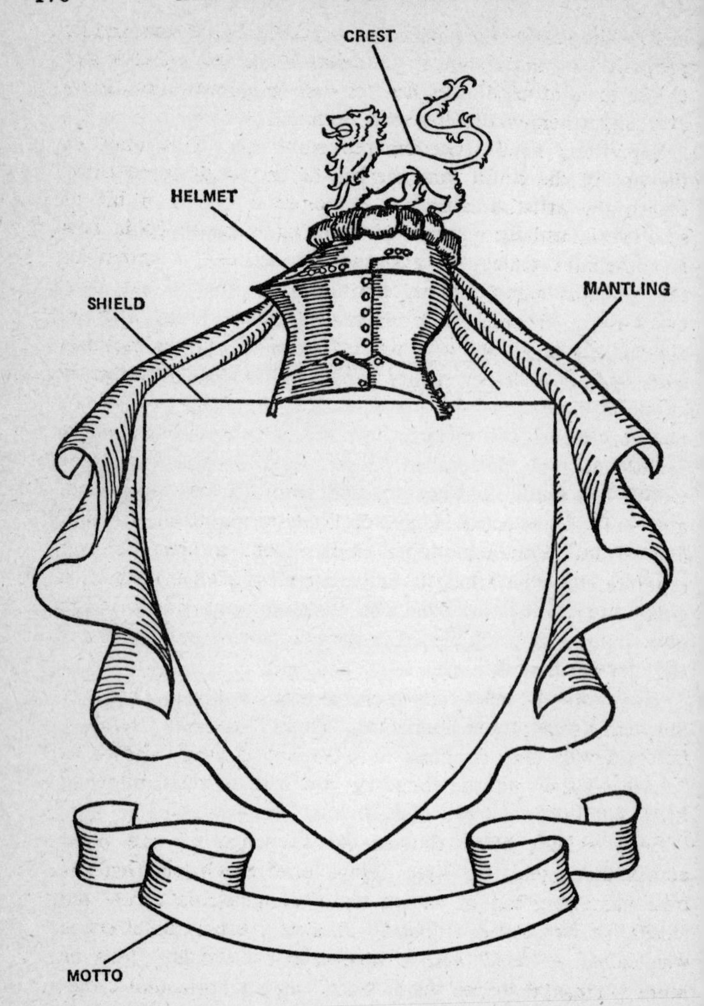

arms with neither helm nor mantling. The wreath under the crest rests directly on the top margin of the shield.

Some arms have "supporters," usually a figure of a person or animal on each side, holding the shield up. However, the supporter in the arms of the United States is the eagle, who carries the shield on his breast. Supporters should properly be granted, and if you assume arms, it is better not to use them at all. In the arms of a state or institution, however, supporters would not be incorrect.

Supporters need something to stand on. This may be the top of the scroll that carries the motto or some other device the artist dreams up. A common one is a bit of scrollwork, usually represented as being made of gold. This is sometimes called a "gas-bracket" because it resembles the wrought metal fixtures that used to hold a gas light away from the wall it hung on. Supporters may also be shown standing on a grassy "compartment" sometimes with badges or other devices scattered on it. A badge is anything that heraldrically symbolizes the owner but is not part of the shield or crest. "E-R" intertwined around a roman numeral "II" makes up one of the royal badges of Queen Elizabeth II. The crowned roses, thistle, shamrock, and daffodil are royal badges of England, Scotland, Ireland, and Wales. You can tell a badge from a crest (shown separate from the arms) because the crest always rests on a wreath or crown, or some other support, while the badge does not. A royal badge may show a crown, but always at the top, not the bottom.

These are the major parts of a coat of arms. The only one that needs any further discussion is the shield. Heraldry books devote long chapters to the many devices, known as "charges," that may be found on a shield, but the following brief outline will get you started.

Early shields often showed just a stripe of one color across the shield. To keep things brief, each one had its own name. Instead of saying "a diagonal stripe across the shield," it was called a "bend." Similarly, a horizontal stripe was called a "fess," and a vertical one a "pale." Two or more horizontal stripes were "bars," and a horizontal crossing a vertical was of course a "cross." A cross with diagonal arms was a "saltire," pronounced either "sal-tire" or "salt ear," and a chevron looked like the insigne of an American army non-commissioned officer. These charges that were not pictures of anything were called "ordinaries."

In addition to ordinaries, the shield could be partitioned into various shapes. For example, a shield divided into bars was called "barry" and "paly" similarly described a shield divided vertically into (usually six) pales. The division could also be along the lines of one of the ordinaries. A shield divided into two colors along the line of a chevron was "per chevron," and so on.

The dividing lines, or the borders of the ordinaries, were not always straight. Sometimes they were "wavy" or scalloped "engrailed," and there were many other forms of partition lines, less common, but each with its own name. These many names were necessary so that a device could be described briefly. If you could not say simply "a cross engrailed," you would have to say "a cross with scallops shaped like a goblet (grail) scooped out of the line all along the edge, with the edges of the scallops meeting in points."

Besides ordinaries and partitions, a shield could show any conceivable bird, beast, plant, or object, including some barely conceivable ones like an "eale" or an "ophiucus." For a complete list, consult the various books on heraldry that you will find in your public library. Charges that pun on the owner's name were very popular. Cockburn bears three cocks and Trumbull three bull's heads. Crosses took dozens of forms, each with its own name, again for brevity. A "cross crosslet fitchy" had smaller crosses at the end of its three top arms, and the bottom arm extended into a point that could be driven into the ground (French *fichee* "drive in").

Additions were often made to arms. If they commemorated some honor they were called "augmentations." The addition made by a cadet to distinguish his arms from the heir's was a "difference." This is also used as a verb; a cadet "differences" his arms, as we have seen.

Arms are also combined or "marshalled" on the same shield. A man would show his arms and those of his wife's father on the same shield. The shield was divided vertically along the line of a pale, so this was called "impaling" the two coats. If an armiger died without male heirs, his arms would vanish unless something was done about it. So his daughter (or daughters) would combine his arms and their sons would bear the father's and mother's arms "quartered." This happened often, and some families inherited dozens or even hundreds of coats. Of course, only a few of these would be shown in any one achievement.

The colors used in heraldry are known as "tinctures." This term includes two "metals," gold and silver, along with five "colors" and a variety of "furs," such as "ermine." The names of the tinctures were derived from the French, as French was the language of the English court when the knights first started to adopt arms. The commoner ones are:

Or: gold, usually shown as yellow
Argent: silver, usually white
Gules: red ("gules" rhymes either with "rules" or "mules," take your choice.)
Azure: blue
Sable: black
Vert: green
Purpure: purple
Proper: in its ordinary colors (a tree "proper" would have a brown stem and green leaves.)

The only fur a beginner needs to consider is "ermine," which is white with black spots representing the black tails of ermine fur. Vert is not one of the commonest colors, and purpure is very rare indeed. It may have been included just to bring the numbers of colors and metals up to the magic seven.

We have talked a lot about brief descriptions of heraldic charges, and these form the basis of blazonry. To "blazon" arms is to describe them briefly but definitely, and "emblazoning" is the opposite—to take the blazon and produce an accurate drawing of it. Blazonry is needed for two reasons, firstly to keep things brief, as we have mentioned under "bend" "cross engrailed", and "cross crosslet fitchy." The other reason is for clarity. Early in the history of arms, the heralds compiled many rolls of arms. These were pictures of the shields and the helmets with their crests, labelled with the names of the owners. This was all they could do at the time, because the rules of blazonry were not fully developed. Besides, in those days only churchmen could read. Blazons of arms are much better than pictures for two reasons. Simple arms can be blazoned in a few short sentences. Books like Burke's or Rietstap's Armorials can list thousands of arms in a small space. Rietstap's *Armorial General* needs only two small volumes to list all the blazons, but it takes a shelf of books for the plates, and these plates show only the shields—no crest or mottoes—in tiny pictures not much bigger than a 35mm slide. A large proportion of them would be meaningless without the blazon to refer to. Rietstap's blazons have been reprinted several times at reasonable cost, but a reprint of the plates today would be priced beyond the reach of any but rich men and the larger libraries.

Another advantage of blazons is their usability. If I come across something I cannot identify in a picture of arms—Rietstap, one of the ancient rolls, or a modern drawing—I am completely at a loss. There is no way of finding out what the beast of object is or how I should draw him. On the other hand, if a blazon mentions a "rustre" or an "alaunt," I can usually resolve my perplexity with an unabridged dictionary, or a complete text of heraldry.

Blazons should be as simple as possible. Before the Victorian and modern reforms of heraldry, blazons had grown unnecessarily complex. Someone invented the "rule" that the same color, charge, or number should never be repeated. This led to the numbering of the colors. If the color of the field (which comes first in any blazon) was gules, then "gules" was never mentioned again. Anything red would have to be described as "of the field" or "of the first." Similarly, if argent was the second tincture, anything silver would be "of the second." By the time a complex blazon got up to the "fourth" or "fifth," even the heralds lost track, and mistakes were bound to be made.

Refusing to name the charge or number a second time also introduced confusion. You would have to distinguish between "on a fess sable, between two roses gules, a crescent argent," and "between two roses or, on a fess sable, a crescent argent." It is much clearer to blazon the first as "a fess sable, between two roses gules, and on the fess a crescent argent," and the other as "a fess sable, with a crescent argent, between two roses or, on the fess." But the rulemakers would eliminate the simpler version, because in each case the word "fess" is repeated.

One problem of blazon is that it leaves a lot to the individual artist. A classic example is the harp for Ireland that is blazoned simply "a harp or, stringed argent." Modern examples of the Royal Arms of England usually show the harp with a perfectly plain post, or with only some simple molding. Earlier versions of the arms, however, show the top of the post decorated with a lion's head or three shamrocks, as well as the more familiar winged woman. None of these is more correct than any other. Any golden harp with silver strings is the emblem of Ireland. Variations in the decoration reflect the taste of the time or even of the individual.

Many other things are left to the taste of the artist. A shield may have almost any outline. Before the Victorian reforms, very complex outlines of the shield were stylish, and the outline would be decorated with curliques and leaves. Today the outline of the shield is usually very plain.

Even when the form of the helmet is dictated by the rank of the wearer, the style is left up to the artist. The complex shield outline was often accompanied by a ridiculous helmet, with a bubble head perched on a skinny neck. The style of the mantling is even freer. Some complexity of the mantling was justified by the explanation that the wear and tear of battle would slit the mantling into many flying ends. Leafy (some would say "spinachy") mantlings were very popular, often with tassels at the end of the major strands. Modern taste in heraldic art is far more toward simplicity of form and outline, but it does not do to be too arbitrary. In years to come ornateness instead of simplicity may again be considered elegant. If anyone is still reading these words, they will then sound hopelessly out of date.

There are many other subjects of heraldry that have been passed over in this brief sketch. The student who would like to go further might best start with Moncrieffe's *Simple Heraldry, Cheerfully Illustrated.* This has been called a "picture book," but it is much more than that. The text is clear and accurate and is an excellent introduction to the subject. Next get Oswald Barron's article on heraldry in the *Encyclopedia Britannica.* It is amply illustrated particularly in the eleventh edition of *Britannica.* This is clear and authoritative and goes a little deeper than Moncreiffe. For the definitive study, look up Fox-Davies' *A Complete Guide to Heraldry.* The original text is rather dated, having appeared over sixty years ago, but the latest edition (1969) revised and annotated by J.P. Brooke-Little, *Richmond Herald,* should be used by every serious student. Fox-Davies and Brooke-Little perhaps overdo the objection to assumed arms. For the opposite position see L.G. Pine's *The Story Of Heraldry.*

One thing remains clear, however: if you want arms of your own to use in the United States, it is perfectly proper to adopt them and start using them. Just be sure they do not infringe on anyone else's arms, and that the design is heraldically good.

11

HEREDITARY, PATRIOTIC, AND GENEALOGICAL SOCIETIES

Ernest F. Kendall

As an amateur genealogist, there are two different (but not mutually exclusive) ways in which you can view the various hereditary, patriotic and genealogical societies. Many people view membership in a certain society as one of the end products of the search; they do their genealogical research in order to find a particular link which makes them eligible to join. An example of this is those who wish to join the Daughters of the American Revolution; they must prove descent from "a man or woman who, with unfailing loyalty to the cause of American Independence, served as a sailor, or as a soldier, or civil officer in one of the several Colonies or States, or in the United Colonies or States, or as a recognized patriot, or rendered material aid thereto."

But another way in which to view the societies is as rich research sources. As, again, in the case of the DAR, many have excellent genealogical libraries, which they permit members and nonmembers alike to use. Many also put out publications which are extremely helpful to anyone engaged in research. In fact, for a number of the organizations listed below, there is no membership requirement beyond a simple interest in genealogy. These organizations (e.g. New England Historic Genealogical Society, New York Genealogical and Biographical Society, Genealogical Society of Pennsylvania) are set up for the primary purpose of collecting and preserving historical and genealogical information, and, as such, have aided countless genealogists in their searches.

The membership requirements of the following societies vary from a very specific genealogical link and an invitation to none at all. The size and scope of their holding and services also vary greatly. Since the best source for detailed information about any organization is that organization itself, we are simply listing the names and addresses of these societies so that you may personally contact any that interest you and obtain complete and up-to-date details.

Children of the Confederacy
328 North Boulevard
Richmond, Virginia 23220

Colonial Dames of America
421 East 61st Street
New York, New York 10021

Dames of the Loyal Legion of the United States
4237 Sansom Street
Philadelphia, Pennsylvania 19104

Descendents of the Illegitimate Sons and Daughters
of the Kings of Britain
℅Brainer T. Peck
Lakeside, Connecticut 06758

Descendents of the Signers of the
Declaration of Independence
℅Historical Society of Pennsylvania
1300 Locust Street
Philadelphia, Pennsylvania 19107

Daughters of the Cincinnati
122 East 58th Street
New York, New York 10022

Daughters of the Republic of Texas
Old Land Office Building
11th and Brazos Streets
Austin, Texas 78701

Genealogical Society of Pennsylvania
1300 Locust Street
Philadelphia, Pennsylvania 19107

Genealogical Society of Colonial Wars
600 Third Avenue
New York, New York 10016

General Society of the Sons of the Revolution
Fraunces Tavern
54 Pearl Street
New York, New York 10004

General Society of the War of 1812
3311 Columbia Pike
Lancaster, Pennsylvania 17603

Heraldry Society
28 Museum Street
London, W.C. 1, England

Hereditary Order of Descendents of Colonial Governors
"Pinecroft"
Harter Road
Morristown, New Jersey

Hood's Texas Brigade Association
Confederate Research Center
Post Office Box 619
Hillsboro, Texas 76645

International Genealogical Club
℅ Baron Jean de Micell
61 rue d'Amsterdam
75-Paris 8, France

Jamestowne Society
4313 North Ashlawn Drive
Richmond, Virginia 23221

Ladies of the Grand Army of the Republic
3515 East Minnehaha Parkway
Minneapolis, Minnesota 55417

Military Order of the Loyal Legion of the United States
1805 Pine Street
Philadelphia, Pennsylvania 19103

National Society of the Children of the
American Revolution
1776 D Street N.W.
Washington, D.C. 20006

National Society of Colonial Dames of America
215 East 71st Street
New York, New York 10021

National Society of the Colonial Dames
of the XVII Century
1300 New Hampshire Avenue, N.W.
Washington, D.C. 20036

National Society of the Colonial Daughters
of the 17th Century
51 King's Highway W.
Haddonfield, New Jersey 08033

National Society of the Daughters of the American Revolution
1776 D Street N.W.
Washington, D.C. 20006

National Society of the Daughters of the Founders
and Patriots of America
1307 New Hampshire Avenue, N.W.
Washington, D.C. 20036

National Society of the Daughters of Utah Pioneers
300 North Main
Salt Lake City, Utah 84103

National Society of New England Women
69 Kensington Road
Bronxville, New York 10708

National Society of the Sons of the American Revolution
2412 Massachusetts Avenue, N.W.
Washington, D.C. 20008

National Society of the Sons and Daughters of the Pilgrims
2714 Green Avenue
Fort Worth, Texas 76109

National Society of the Sons of Utah Pioneers
2998 Connor Street (2150 East)
Salt Lake City, Utah 84109

National Society of the United States Daughters of 1812
℅ Mrs. Ira J. Dietrich
1421 E. 19th Street
Tulsa, Oklahoma 74120

National Society of Women Descendents of the Ancient
and Honorable Artillery Company

3627 Chesapeake Street, N.W.
Washington, D.C. 20008

National Woman's Relief Corps
(Auxiliary to the Grand Army of the Republic)
629 South Seventh
Springfield, Illinois 62703

New England Historic Genealogical Society
101 Newbury Street
Boston, Massachusetts 02116

New York Genealogical and Biographical Society
122 East 58th Street
New York, New York 10022

Order of Colonial Lords of Manors in America
℅ Robert D.L. Gardiner
230 Park Avenue
New York, New York 10017

Order of First Families of Virginia, 1607-1624
℅ Mrs. Herbert D. Forrest
747 Euclid Avenue
Jackson, Mississippi 39202

Order of the Founders and Patriots of America
℅ Federal Hall Memorial
15 Pine Street
New York, New York 10005

Order of the Stars and Bars
Southern Station
Post Office Box 1
Hattiesburg, Mississippi 39401

Pennsylvania German Society
R.D. 1
Breinigsville, Pennsylvania 18031

Pilgrim Society
Pilgrim Hall Museum
Plymouth, Massachusetts 02360

Scotch-Irish Society of the United States of America
2301 Packard Building
Philadelphia, Pennsylvania 19102

Society of the Ark and the Dove
℅ The Maryland Historical Society

201 West Monument Street
Baltimore, Maryland 21201

Society of the Cincinnati
2118 Massachusetts Avenue, N.W.
Washington, D.C. 20008

Society of Genealogists
37 Harrington Gardens
London, SW 7-4JX, England

Society of the War of 1812 in the
Commonwealth of Pennsylvania
% Russel Bement, Jr.
108 Avon Road
Haverford, Pennsylvania 19041

Society of the Whiskey Rebellion of 1794
Dallowgill
3311 Columbia Pike
Lancaster, Pennsylvania 17603

Sons of Confederate Veterans
Southern Station, Box 1
Hattiesburg, Mississippi 39401

Sons and Daughters of Pioneer Rivermen
121 River Avenue
Sewickley, Pennsylvania 15143

Sons of Union Veterans of the Civil War
Post Office Box 24
Gettysburg, Pennsylvania 17325

Sons of Union Veterans of the Civil War Auxiliary
5137 North Howard Street
Philadelphia, Pennsylvania

St. Nicholas Society of the City of New York
122 East 58th Street
New York, New York 10022

Unitarian and Universalist Genealogical Society
3608 Clifmar Road
Baltimore, Maryland 21207

United Daughters of the Confederacy
328 North Boulevard
Richmond, Virginia 23220

BIBLIOGRAPHY

Babbel, June Andrew, comp. *Lest We Forget: A Guide to Genealogical Research in the Nation's Capital.* 3rd ed. Annandale, Virginia: Potomac Stake of the Church of Jesus Christ of Latter-day Saints, 1969.

Bailey, Thomas A. *The American Spirit: United States History as Seen by Contemporaries.* vol. 1. Boston: D.C. Heath & Co., 1963.

Barck, Oscar, Theodore, Jr., and Lefler, Hugh Talmage. *Colonial America.* New York: The Macmillan Co., 1958.

Barron, Arthur Oswald. "Heraldry." In *Shakespeare's England.* Oxford: Clarendon Press, 1916.

Blum, John M., et al. *The National Experience: A History of the United States.* 2nd ed. New York: Harcourt, Brace & World, 1968.

Boutell, Charles. *Boutell's Heraldry.* Edited by C.W. Scott-Giles and J.P. Brooke-Little. 5th ed. London: Warne, 1966.

Burke, (John) Bernard. *The General Armory of England, Scotland, Ireland and Wales.* London: Harrison, 1878.

Child, Heather. *Heraldric Design: A Handbook for Students.* London: G. Bell and Sons, 1965.

Colket, Meredith B., Jr., and Bridgers, Frank E. *Guide to Genealogical Records in the National Archives.* National Archives Publication No. 64-8. Washington, D.C.: National Archives and Records Service, 1964.

Daniel, J.R.V. *A Hornbook of Virginia History.* Richmond: The Virginia Department of Conservation and Development, 1949.

Doane, Gilbert H. *Searching for Your Ancestors: The How and Why of Genealogy.* 3rd ed. Minneapolis: University of Minnesota Press, 1960.

Encyclopedia of Associations. Detroit: Gale Research Co., 1972.

Everton, George B., Sr., ed. *The Handy Book for Genealogists.* 6th rev. ed. Logan, Utah: Everton Publishers, 1791.

Fairbairn, James. *Crests of the Families of Great Britain.* 2 vols. 4th ed. London: Jack, 1905.

Filby, P. William, comp. *American and British Genealogy and Heraldry, a Selected List of Books.* Chicago: American Library Assoc., 1970.

Fox-Davies, A.C. *A Complete Guide to Heraldry.* Revised and annotated by J.P. Brooke-Little. London: Thomas Nelson and Sons, Ltd., 1969.

Gayre, Robert. *Heraldic Standards and Other Ensigns.* Edinburgh: Oliver and Boyd, 1959.

Hansen, Marcus Lee. *The Atlantic Migration, 1607-1860.* Cambridge: Harvard University Press, 1951.

Hassall, W.O. *History Through Surnames.* Oxford, England: Pergamon Press, 1967.

Hawke, David. *The Colonial Experience.* New York: Bobbs-Merrill Co., 1966.

Innes, Thomas, of Learney. *Scots Heraldry: A. . . Handbook on the Historical Principles and Modern Applications of the Art and Science.* 2nd ed. Edinburgh: Oliver and Boyd, 1956.

Jacobus, Donald L. *Genealogy as Pastime and Profession.* 2nd ed. Baltimore: Genealogical Publishing Co., 1968.

Jones, Maldwyn Allen. *American Immigration.* Chicago: University of Chicago Press, 1967.

Kennedy, John F. *A Nation of Immigrants.* New York: Harper & Row, 1964.

Kephart, Calvin. *Origin of Heraldry in Europe.* 3rd ed. Baltimore: Heraldic Book Co., 1964.

Matthews, Constance M. *English Surnames.* New York: Charles Scribner's Sons, 1967.

Moncreiffe, Iain, and Pottinger, Don. *Simple Heraldry.* Edinburgh: Nelson Press, 1953.

Papworth, John W., and Morant, Alfred W. *An Alphabetical Dictionary of Coats of Arms . . . Ordinary of British Armorials.* Reprint with introduction by G.D. Squibb and A.R. Wagner. London: Tabard Publications, 1961.

Parker, James, publ. *Glossary of the Terms Used in Heraldry.* New edition. Oxford: 1894.

Paul, James B. *Ordinary of Scottish Arms.* Edinburgh: Green, 1903.

Pine, Leslie Gilbert. *The Story of Heraldry.* London: County Life, Ltd., 1952.

Puttock, A.G. *Dictionary of Heraldry and Related Subjects.* Baltimore: Genealogical Publishing Co., 1970.

Rietstap, J.B. *Armorial General.* 2nd ed. 1884. Reprinted in 2 vols. London: Heraldry Today, 1965.

Rubincam, Milton, and Stephenson, Jean, eds. *Genealogical Research Methods and Sources.* Washington, D.C.: American Society of Genealogists, 1966.

Schultz, Harold John. *History of England.* New York: Barnes & Noble, 1968.

Stephenson, Jean. *Heraldry for the American Genealogist.* Special publication no. 25. Washington, D.C.: National Genealogical Society, 1959.

Stevenson, Noel C. *Search and Research: The Researcher's Handbook.* rev. ed. Salt Lake City: Deseret Book Co., 1959.

Thompson, Henry F. "An Atlantic Voyage in the Seventeenth Century." *Maryland Historical Magazine* 2(1907).

Tunis, Edwin. *Colonial Living.* Cleveland: The World Publishing Co., 1957.

Whitehill, Walter Muir. *Independent Historical Societies.* Boston: The Boston Athenaeum, 1962.

Williams, Ethel W. *Know Your Ancestors: A Guide to Genealogical Research.* Rutland, Vermont: C.E. Tuttle Co., 1960.

Zabriskie, George O. *Climbing Our Family Tree Systematically.* Salt Lake City: Parliament Press, 1969.